The Lion's Mouth

Prose Series 16

Caterina Edwards

The Lion's Mouth

A Novel

Guernica

Montreal/New York, 1993

The first edition was published by NeWest Publishers 1982.
First published in this format in 1993 by Guernica Editions.

Antonio D'Alfonso, editor
Guernica Editions Inc.
P.O. Box 633, Station N.D.G.
Montreal (Quebec), Canada H4A 3R1

Guernica Editions Inc.
340 Nagel Drive
Cheektowaga, N.Y. 14225-4731 USA

Legal Deposit — Second Quarter
National Library of Canada
and Bibliothèque nationale du Québec

Canadian Cataloguing in Publication Data

Edwards, Caterina, 1948-
The lion's mouth

(Prose series; 16)
New ed.
ISBN 0-920717-67-5

I. Title. II. Series.

PS8559.D83L58 1993 C813'.54 C'92-090733-4
PR9199.3.E39L56 1993

I would like to thank Gary Watson for his insightful reading and concrete help and Rudy Wiebe for years of support and guidance. I would also like to thank Antha van Herk for her valuable reading of the final draft of the manuscript and Alberta Culture and The Canada Council for their financial assistance.

Caterina Edwards

For M.P.L., with love

La Falsita non dico mai mai
ma la verita non a ognuno.

(I never, never tell a lie
But the Truth not to everyone.)

Carlo Goldoni

Da Venezie lontan da mile mia
No passa di che no ne venga in menta
Il dolce nome de la patria mia
Il Lenguaze e i costume de la zente.

(From Venice, I am far a thousand miles
But a day does not pass that the sweet
Name of my country does not come to mind
The language and the costumes of my people.)

Carlo Goldoni

There is nothing more to be said about it. Everyone has been there and everyone has brought back a collection of photographs.

Henry James in his introduction to
Venice, a Portrait

Prologue

My hands are covered with small scratches, the dirt embedded under my nails and in the cracks. The rest of me is sticky with sweat, suntan lotion, and insect repellent. I have spent the morning gardening, uprooting thistles and chickweed from between the zucchini and lettuce plants, hacking back a wild rosebush and the Virginia creeper. I am floating in self-righteousness, in the image of myself as establisher of order, shaper of boundaries.

On the way to the bath, I check the mail box. Your mother's letter waits, between my *New Yorker* and *NeWest Review*. It was mailed exactly four months ago. Italian and Canadian postal services, plus a casual strike, have produced the usual level of efficiency; I toss the letter down. Better to wait until I'm cool and clean, iced drink in hand. But after one step, I turn back. Your mother's letters are always more duty than relaxation. If I don't make myself read it now, the envelope could be on my coffee table for weeks. It is not that I do not welcome news of you, of Tarquinio and Lea and all your families. I welcome and I await. But my dear aunt's letters, no matter the content, repel in form and tone. She covers each inch of tissue-thin paper with what seems, to my Canadian eyes, illegible handwriting. (Though, to be fair, she finds my standard school script bizarre and aberrant.) She scorns punctuation, the sentences tumble, gasp, and sputter across the page. And the voice behind those poor sentences, need I tell you, pours out, complains, bemoans: endlessly.

But this time, as I scan the letter for a nugget of information, I discover more than I expected.

'*Bianca, se sapessi, se sapessi,*' if you knew, if you knew. '*Che disgrazia di Dio.*' God's disgrace? I must be translating incorrectly, a disgrace from God. '*Barbara scossa.*' Barbara has been shocked? hit? shaken? 'She saw what she shouldn't have seen and now she fears everything. Damned brigadists.' Typically, my aunt does not explain further; there is no hint as to the source of the shock, the content of the fear. 'Worse, Marco (you, you) suffered a nervous breakdown.' *Esaurimento nervoso*, the words translated literally as an exhaustion of the nerves. How controlled and nineteenth century-ish it sounds. Your mother has been decrying the state of your nerves for years. But this time it is serious. You had to be hospitalized. Had to be. Melodramatic pictures flash through my mind: locks, bars, burly attendants. And, almost as quickly, I am casting myself in the role of champion — discovering the hidden path, the hidden door, rescuing you from your fortress of self, guiding you back to the world.

Paola refuses to visit you or let Francesco see you. Your mother continues to beg, reminding Paola of her wifely duty, of your need. It does no good. Paola insists Francesco must not be disturbed, must not be contaminated by seeing the depth of your collapse. She goes so far as to suggest that you wished it all upon your son; you endangered him.

'I imagine if this could be true?' Your mother's last sentences are written up and down the small margins in miniscule handwriting. 'But what is the truth, that I don't know. I am old, every second older. And I know only that my son is not getting better. He's suspended.'

I am hot and cold; my skin stands up in goose bumps. It is as if you are suddenly in the room with me. I sense you close behind me, just out of reach. But at the same time, I am overwhelmed by the distance between us. My mind paraphrases a half-remembered sentence of Henry James. Mile after mile of ocean, province after dreadful province, between us. I am helpless before such separation.

What could I do for you even if I were there in Venice? Try to beg Paola myself? Kidnap Francesco and bring him to you? Stand by you, certainly, but I want to do more. I want to be the one who not only knows but illuminates

11

the truth. I want to tell your story. In the top drawer of the filing cabinet in the basement, there are three attempts at a novel, three attempts at understanding, at explaining you, three attempts that trail off into shallowness, falsity.

I wash my hands with lavender-scented soap. I soak my wrists in cool water. It is time again to lift the pen. It is time to succeed.

Afternoon

I

He was drawn to the window like an addict
to his source. As soon as he stepped into
Adolfo's office, he felt the pull. He felt himself
edging toward the glass, upholding his part of
the discussion, pausing to finger his boss's col-
lection of antique carnival masks, to stroke the
skinlike dark leather, the fragile lace, but still
edging, edging. One short step from the end
of the brass bookcase and he had reached the
broad window ledge. The view was his, laid
out for his needful eye.

'It's not the type of opportunity that comes
along every day. Either for the department or
for you.'

'True.'

'They were impressed with your remodel-
ling of *El Convento* so they asked specifically
for you. It would involve going to Geneva for
a few weeks of consultation, of course.'

'I don't know if I could go . . .'

'I'm sure we could arrange it so you could
have a couple of weeks at — say — St. Moritz.
One of our best suites, all expenses covered.
I've heard you're a great skier.'

'I used to be.'

'I don't understand your lack of enthusiasm. Surely your wife could take some time off.'

It had stopped raining. A few feeble rays of late afternoon sun had broken through the clouds to light up the wet piazza and the double image of the dominating church; a floating apparition gleaming as if cut from shot silk. The *campanile*, however, was solid, heavily real, its reflection a simple long band of shadow. Again, the glimpse of palace behind appeared ethereal, a pink and white fantasy. How well it masked the inner warren of rooms and dungeons that was once the city's core of power, guarded by a gate of stone lions and protected by the essential lion: *la bocca di leone* — the mouth for secret denunciations.

'The whole family could benefit from the mountain air, I would think.' Adolfo was smiling his crooked toothed smile, his smug, well-fed body comfortably relaxed in the massive black leather chair as if unaware of how uneasy his words made Marco.

'If I had this office, I'd never get any work done.'

'It fades.'

'I've lived in Venice most of my life and it's never faded for me. Each time, it's just as wondrous.'

Adolfo swivelled his leather chair around to glance out of the window. 'Actually if you're

right about yourself you'll never get this office.'
He was exposing even more crooked teeth.

Marco, with a last look at the shimmering piazza, moved himself to the low plush sofa opposite Adolfo's. He wasn't sure what his boss meant. The facial expression was friendly but there was a tinge of criticism, an undertone of threat to the words. Marco allowed his face an ironical twist. 'I do know I'm happy with my position . . . in life. I've never aspired to certain heights or certain views.' Not, he wished he could say, bcause of a lack of competence. You are proof that incompetence and a small mind are the best requisites for a 'certain position' in life.

The folds of Adolfo's face dropped into a serious expression. He leaned across the desk, his chemical smell lunging like an invisible extension encircling Marco's throat and causing a sudden difficulty in breathing. 'You didn't answer me before about taking your family. Or do you Venetians scorn setting foot on terra firma?'

'It's always complicated trying to travel, but now . . . it's impossible. You must understand.'

'Then you'll go alone?'

'I don't like leaving them.'

'Perhaps you don't realize the full situation.' Adolfo let his stocky finger fall on one of the intercom buttons. 'Daniela . . . ask Mr. Raponi to come and see me now.'

Marco tried again. 'I thought you understood that I had more than personal reasons for not wanting to work on this project. I've stated before that I am totally opposed to the idea of a new resort complex on the Lido.'

'You're right. I don't understand. Not at all. Though I should have foreseen this. We seem to hold divergent views on everything lately. But I thought this time . . . Well, firstly, I presumed you would jump at the chance to begin on the ground floor, to begin with tabula rasa, to design without constraints of what was. Not to be confined to remodelling, to tinkering with swimming pools, to lay the foundations —'

'Tabula Rasa? After the bulldozers are finished.'

'Secondly, you must see that the Lido is dead. A cadaver. It needs —'

'It doesn't need to be turned into another Jesolo, so many people you can't even see the sand, tacky apartment buildings . . . Lido may be *démodé* . . .'

Marco was interrupted by a timid knock. The door opened to a round, big-eyed, clown face. 'May I?'

'Please, Nanni, come in.'

Adolfo directed Nanni to pull a wooden chair to a point to the right of Adolfo's desk so they faced Marco together. Both were overweight, complacent, but in Adolfo these elements were molded into a bulky self-centredness: his large grey head, his silk-suited shoulders dominated space, whereas in Raponi the weight and attitude sank into a smug flabbiness; his round cheeks pulled into a perpetual nice-guy smile, his round belly strained against his too tight jacket.

'Our dear leftist friend here,' Adolfo was addressing Raponi, 'great defender of unions, strikes and the common man, wants to keep the best beach on the Adriatic exclusively for the rich, besides scorning all the jobs.' They were both emitting the chemical smell. Trying to analyse what it was, Marco stopped listening. It was only when the phrase 'pure and modern' poked through his concentration that he recognized the assaulting odour as the popular cologne Vidal's *Pino* — an artificial reproduction of the scent of pine trees. 'Evoke the pure outdoors,' the commercial sang as a forest shrank into the shape of a green glass pine needle with a gold metal top.

Raponi began playing the role for which he had been cast. 'Well, if Marco isn't interested, there are people, as I was telling you, in my division who would love to take over this project. Giacomo has already begun preliminary sketches He has an exciting idea for a central building of "flying saucer" design encircled by glass towers.' Adolfo's strategies were the same every time. He started with a personal appeal, he avoided even acknowledging any attendant moral issues, he switched to ridicule and then played one person off against another. He knew well what Marco thought of Giacomo's abilities or Raponi's entire division, for that matter.

'Jesolo is only twenty kilometres away . . .'

'You must see, the project will go ahead. We aren't speaking of a few lire here or a few jobs. So the only question that remains is whether you will give your input.' Adolfo continued on and on, stretching the only question into something oblique and unfathomable. When continually met with firmness his last strategy was a confusing disintegration. As he spoke, his face was contorted into a fierce frown so that as Marco gazed from him to the smiling Raponi he had the feeling he was facing not two human faces but the theatre masks of comedy and tragedy. With a few last references to Marco's 'superior talents' and 'ability to work out a compromise perfect for all parties', Adolfo was finished. He had used all his tricks in trying to convince Marco, to persuade, as if he didn't know that, in the end, just as in all their previous disagreements, Marco would have to give in, would have to submit. The knowledge was kept hovering on the outskirts of the scene, adding a subtle tang to Adolfo's bullying tone. After all, it implied, how many architectural jobs were there in Venice or even the surrounding area? After all, what choice do you have? You work for us or you don't work.

'Who would you say was Venice's greatest architect?'

Suspiciously Raponi offered, 'Palladio?'

'Yes, of course.' Marco lifted himself from the sofa and crossed back to the window. The view soothed, strengthened. 'Did you know he had a great plan to tear down the *Doge's* palace and build a new one, more pure, more classical, better designed. It was almost carried out. Now we can see what a disaster that would have been, what we would have lost. You make fun of my concern. But think about what you want to do. Turn the *grande dame* of resorts into another cheap . . . I can appreciate the arguments for the plan — the need for employment. I see she's out of step, out of favour, but she was out of 'style' in Mann's day. She is what she is. It's like those who'd pave the Grande Canal to bring Venice into the twentieth century. It's murder.'

Marco congratulated himself, on his way back to his own desk, for managing to deliver the speech he had been harbouring for some time. Still, he had held himself back. He hadn't told them that their 'international modern' was what was 'out of style', was what was 'corpse-like'. They could never admit to that. The style was the natural expression of the multinational corporation they worked for; it spoke, it communicated authority. And yet, by now, Adolfo and Raponi would be accusing Marco of elitism, of not wanting people to benefit from sea air, if they hadn't already gone on to his more private flaws.

He was pulling on his coat when Adolfo suddenly appeared at his door. 'How about coming out for dinner with me? My treat. *La Colomba?* You look like you could use a good meal.'

'No, I don't think . . .'

Adolfo moved in closer. 'I know your wife is in Padova with your little boy tonight. You don't have that excuse and, as it happens, mine's away too. In the mountains. So we could make a night of it. Two free men, hey? I phoned Marcella. Remember, I told you about her, works in the pharmacy on San Toma.'

'I have seen her.'

'She has a friend she can bring along that's a real — let me say, she's well made, she's . . .'

Marco edged away from Adolfo toward the door. He could almost see the saliva pooling in his boss's mouth. 'I must go. I promised my brother that I'd eat with them.'

'You are a family man. Why don't you call them, tell them you have to work late? I'm sure their kitchen can't compare to that of *La Colomba.* Have you ever tried its squid and polenta? Exquisite. Marcella and her friend. What do you say?'

'My stomach . . . I'm not much of an eater.' Especially not, Marco added to himself, escaping at last down the corridor, around you.

II

The vision of a saucer and tower resort dropped into the middle of the fading elegance of the Lido propelled Marco down the *calle*. Idiots — they swept out memory and variety with impunity. Dangerous idiots, with small stones instead of hearts. He imagined Raponi and Adolfo dressed in prison-striped garb, each chained to a great broom. A little forced labour would do them good, cut into their smugness and fat, a little sweeping out of the wastes. Push that broom. Lift that dirt. Appropriate.

Seeing the floating station for the *vaporetto* before him, Marco realized he had been going in the wrong direction, towards home instead of towards Calore's jewelry shop. It was Paola's birthday in three days and, with her away in Padova, today was the logical day for present-buying. As he pushed his way back through the commuter crowd, he understood that he had been wrong about the direction of his emotions too. It was not anger, which would have enabled him to float over the rush of faceless people, wearers of musky perfume, leather and furs in a universal desire, it seemed, for an animal persona. It was the old anxiety returning.

The muscles around his head, behind his eyes, across his chest and abdomen were tight, clenched as if three steel bands had suddenly locked in place, cutting off all connections. Leaving isolation.

At least this time he could attribute some cause. Padova. His son. So small and who more helpless?

'There is a slight mortality rate from this procedure.' Doctor Lambrusco had said the words casually. 'And, of course, the rate is a bit higher for children.'

Marco stopped before the window of a lingerie store. Delicate crimson nightgowns of silk and lace had been arranged around a core picture of a naked woman. Briefly, he considered surprising Paola. But she would be embarrassed; it would be too unexpected, too intimate. No, jewelry was best, like all other years. Another gold bracelet or gold chain to add to the hoard. 'Your armour,' he called it. And she would laugh and move away, jangling and formidable.

She was good with the doctors, pushing for the proper explanation, the proper care. While he with his distaste was useless, as she pointed out.

Those white, masked men bending over that small body, as they had once bent over him.

His muscles relaxed slightly in a sudden rush of gratitude to Paola. 'There's no need for us both to go this time.' She had under-stood his difficulty. He resolved to buy her something special.

Those white, masked men. Cold-eyed. Last time in Padova, Francesco had burst into tears when they had simply walked into the room. Burst into tears and stretched his arms out to his father. Marco had held the soft, pudgy body close. 'It's all right. Daddy's here. He won't let anyone hurt you. Daddy's here.' Wondering, as always, if Francesco had any idea of what the words meant. For if his son did understand, he would also soon understand that the words were lies — nothing was right and his father had no protective power. Particularly not from the cold-eyed men who evaluated deficiencies.

'We will be entering through the femoral artery.'

'Femoral?' Paola had immediately inter-rupted.

'The artery in the groin.'

'The weak spot of us all.' Marco attempted wit to dissipate the heaviness in the white, sun-bright office, the heaviness forming in his stomach.

'The catheter is pushed up the artery until we reach the aorta.'

'The heart of the matter.' It was a mutter, barely audible. Paola, each tired line, each in-cipient wrinkle highlighted in the sun, shot him one of her glances.

'We inject the dye, first into the left ventricle. This enables us to see if the dye leaks, in other words, if there is a hole. We can check each valve for pressure, and also we can determine the shape and size of the heart.'

Nothing was closed, nothing private. The cold-eyed men saw all.

'But you know that there's a hole already.' Paola was leaning forward, one ringed hand clutching the edge of the supermodern metal desk. 'You said the blood shunts back and forth . . .'

'As I said — from the symptoms — the fainting, the turning blue, the inability to withstand any exertion. It is a common problem in children of his sort.'

'So the test?'

'The cardiac angiography is necessary to enable us to decide if an operation is worthwhile.'

Worthwhile to whom? What kind of life was necessary before it was judged worth preserving?

Marco paused at the top of the Rialto to catch his breath. Unconsciously, he had been walking faster and faster, almost running up the steps. He glanced to his right up the Grande Canale. Twilight — there was an amethyst haze over the base green and grey. The shops and stalls had turned on their lights, lining the bridge with a golden glow. The crowd here was thicker. People crossed back and forth, forcing him to dodge and weave. Laden with market purchases, as they called out to each other, they waved string bags filled with lemons and paper-wrapped fish. One woman, darting in front of him to capture and then shake her escaping child, hit his arm with some very hard apples. '*Figlio mio*,' my son, she screeched, almost in Marco's ear. Then, noticing his wince and effort to get around her and her son, 'Eyyyii, children! What can you expect?' she yelled after him.

Marco hadn't thought himself a child on that day when they had bent over him under the dazzling lights. Cutting and opening, their rubberized fingers plunging deep. Fourteen years old. But now he saw that he had been a child and that day had been a type of reverse initiation rite. Instead of snipping away foreskin, they had taken most of his stomach. Though he knew it was foolish, he always felt they had left a hole, that when the anxiety descended, the emptiness at his centre was physical as well as emotional.

The cold-eyed men. How easily they plunged into the mystery of man behind his skin. Still, that was where man was simplest. In appearances and actions we are most varied. Inside, we are alike. One cell like another, one liver like another, one heart. Only in abnormality was there individuality. The abnormality of Francesco who differed in something so minute as a chromosome. His defective son. The seed of his emptiness.

He had seen, oh yes, he'd seen inside. Blood, a strangely warm rain in the cold November air. The bodies split. Gashed. Hanging above him. Still fresh and hot. He knew. He could see. Blood on the dirt, on the grass, on his face.

He couldn't breathe. The pain across his chest was unbearable. Gulping air, Marco doubled over, one arm going out to the *calle* wall for support. As his hand touched the wet paper of the poster, he began to grow calmer, forcing himself to take deep breaths. He wasn't four years old. He wasn't in Zara. The family had come to Venice, to safety. They'll never bomb Venice.

He must watch himself. He hadn't remembered for so long. He must have slipped up, somehow allowed the images out of their lair. He traced his fingers over the black block letters on the poster. The artisans of Venice were calling for a general strike to demand that their city be saved.

Calore was waiting on two American tourists, but as soon as Marco entered, he called back through the doorway behind him to his wife. 'Maria. A coffee, immediately.'

Marco sat on a small velvet chair in the corner of the shop farthest away from the main counter. The tourist couple were dressed in matching black leather trench coats which, since both were tall and hefty, seemed to fill the small shop: dark, shiny, and ominous.

Marco bent his head and shaded his eyes with his hand to block out the sight and all its connotations. He had to be careful.

Maria brought the espresso in a graceful mauve cup on a silver tray. 'Drink up. You look awfully pale.' She stood over him, an elegant middle-aged woman, grey-haired in grey silk. He finished the thick, bitter coffee in a gulp.

'Not a good day.'

'I can see that. The weather is nasty, isn't it?'

'The water is high.'

'You're here for your wife's present? Domini will be finished in a minute but, if you like, I could show you.'

'No. I'm in no rush. Americans?'

'French-Canadians, I think they said. They're certainly buying. For him too. Chains, pendants, rings.'

Their eyes met in humour. 'It's the coats, I can't look at them without . . .'

'Bad memories for all of us. But you must have been a baby. I'm surprised you can remember anything.'

The couple had finally bought enough. When they went out the door, laden with small packages, the shop immediately seemed three times larger. Calore smiled at Marco. 'That was a bit difficult. Speaking English was a strain for both sides and we couldn't understand each other's French.'

'Difficult but profitable.'

'Ah, profitable.' Calore shrugged his shoulders. 'I manage. And you? You seem . . .'

'Life grows ever more complicated. But, at the moment, I'm interested in something special, truly special, for my wife. I saw her inspecting an ad for diamond stud earrings.'

Back in role, Calore was already bending over behind the counter for the diamond earring tray, already muttering, 'Very fashionable, very today.'

'No.' Maria returned from the back room where she had taken the cup and tray. 'Signora Mazzin has been in several times. It's not the earrings that she wants. She was most clear in her interests.'

It was a beautiful ring: a square-cut, deep blue sapphire, encircled by diamonds. As he turned the ring under the light, he understood from the size of the demand the depth of Paola's discontent.

Evening

III

It was darker now. The edges (doorways, corners, the short arcades that ended in blank walls) were impenetrably black.

'Struggle occurs in any marriage.' At a family dinner back at the beginning of the marriage, back before Francesco, his brother Tarquinio had lectured.

'You feel I should take charge in the old-fashioned way. Rule the roost.' Paola was not with him, having preferred a television spectacular to his family.

'You know I'm not suggesting that. You must struggle for a balance.'

'But the irritation . . .'

'I'm saying it's there for everyone, but it's cyclical. It appears, collects and evaporates. Under the sun of love. Only to appear again. A cycle.' Tarquinio had smiled in satisfaction at his latest of metaphors.

But Paola's discontent had only deepened. And he had stood aside and avoided sounding its depths.

'If you don't take that expression off your face and start looking as if you were a part of all this, this marriage is off, ceremony or no ceremony,' she whispered, not five minutes after they had been pronounced man and wife.

They stood in front of the side altar of the Immaculate Conception in the church of San Pantaleon. The photographer was trying to pose them by that dark ikon so that they would manage to look both madly in love and ir-reproachingly devout. The wedding guests were watching, offering advice. It was decided that the picture would be taken with Marco on one side of the mosaic, hands clasped but not elevated, and Paola on the other, her arm extended, her hand in the act of laying the ex-pensive bouquet of white baby roses on the altar as an offering.

There was still some debate between their respective mothers as to whether the fading bouquets of the brides married earlier in the week should be removed. Paola whispered. The picture was taken, and they were eternal-ized. He had tried to adjust his expression which, if it matched his inner feelings, was one of embarrassment, but he succeeded only in looking split, an ugly, amused face floating over an awkward body. Whereas the image of herself Paola gave to posterity was that of a magazine cover bride. So perfect in her elegant lace and silk, in the pearl coronet and the cas-cading floor length veil. She glowed, yes, but her head was lifted in anger and gave any viewer of the picture no sense of maidenly modesty or devotion.

'*Stasera mi butto.*' The silly pop song they had danced to so unrestrainedly the summer before the wedding played itself over and over in his mind. His feet hit the pavement, echoing the primitive beat of Italian imitation rock. Gradually, the clicks of leather on asphalt grew more muffled, squishy. Stopping at the top of a bridge and gazing down at the twisting *calle*, he saw the last of the evening crowd; no longer merely insulated by hats and scarves, by closely held bags and high boots, they hurried along heads bent, black umbrellas extended. Still, it was only when he turned to the canal and saw the broken surface of the green water that he realized it was raining again. Suddenly, he was aware that his hair was unpleasantly wet, that water was seeping down his neck, that his collar was damp and tight.

He began running, pushing his way down the *calle*, then turning off down a narrow, empty *fondamento*. *Stasera*. *Stasera*. Tonight, tonight. Quickly, he was out of air. Slowing, he glimpsed at the end of a narrow path branching off to the left the bright lights of a café.

It was a neighbourhood café: plain wooden tables and chairs, the strong perfume of coffee and sweet liqueur. The foremost decoration was the bar itself: two shelves of glittering bottles, two of glass jars filled with multi-coloured candy, the silver coffee machine and, beneath the counter, tray after tray of tiny pastries.

Elbowing his way through the tight crowd of eating and drinking patrons standing in front of the bar, he managed to catch the barman's attention and order a double espresso. Then, shaking out his coat, surveying the mostly empty tables, he saw her. She sat in a corner smoking, her face almost deliberately empty of expression. Elena.

'May I join you?'

There was a flash, beneath the surface but visible. It was enough to concentrate her beauty. It was no longer the beauty she had when they were children. Elena had been like a precious gem — clear and perfectly formed. Both men and women turned to stare when she appeared. No. But neither was she like the last time they had met on the Piazza. In front of the perfection of the church and the square, her greyness had been a shock. He had seen only the lines forming around her mouth and her eyes, the haphazardness of her paint, the dullness of her once golden hair. No. Today her smile cut through the wet and cold.

'It's been a long time.'

'Yes. I don't remember when?'

'That demonstration. You and your friends were occupying St. Mark's square.' He motioned to the barman to bring over his coffee. 'Sleeping on cots. To emphasize the lack of living space in Venice for the poor.'

'What a clever boy. You read the placards.'

Her face was opening. 'They tried everything to get us out.'

'You did tend to harangue the tourists.'

'They tried everything. So bad for the romantic view of Venice you know. Everything except giving in. Everything except doing something with those deserted, rotting palaces.'

'Exactly. I have to deal with it every day. Even if it were cheaper to renovate here they would still rather throw up yet another concrete block in Mestre. So much neater, you know, purer. Makes me ill . . . So, how are you doing? From what I've noted, you didn't have much success.'

'Oh, I've given all that up. You're right. One doesn't get any results. They don't listen.'

'You have given up politics? I don't believe you.'

'No. No. No.' She lit a new cigarette with the end of her first one. 'Just that kind of thing. Demonstrations are too unproductive. One must —' Her eyes shifted from the blank wall back to Marco and she stopped suddenly. 'But how are you? Besides thinner than ever?'

'Surviving.'

Her hair was in a fuzz around her face now. She had worn it long, in two thick, bright braids. Once, caught by the pincers of stomach pain, lying on the living room sofa, those two braids hanging over him, almost touching his face. Her face farther away, but concerned. 'Marco, what can I do?'

'Bell ropes,' his brother used to call them. 'Bell ropes, if I pull them does your head go ding dong?' She would jerk her head away, call him idiot, but her eyes were pleased, shining whenever Tarquinio deigned to speak to her.

'And Tarquinio?' It was always one of her first questions when their families both lived in the Palazzo Morosini. (Her parents, working for the Morosinis as butler and housekeeper, had the superior roof apartment. His, in their financial embarrassment, managed to rent part of the damp and odorous main floor.) When she descended through the glamorous middle stories to share homework or play, while still on the doorstep, she would ask: 'And Tarquinio?'

'He's a bit worried about his job. If this last Russian contract isn't renewed, and it looks as if it won't, the situation will be difficult. Still, on a personal level, he is — as he puts it — a flourishing bay tree, all glossy and green with health.'

'No more talk of emigration?'

'No. He's had enough of that. Too deeply rooted here, really. Seriously, he is happy. As happy as I have ever seen him.'

She ran her fingers through her curls and grimaced. 'Oh, Marco, it's impossible to be flourishing on a personal level, only on that level. You should know that. And politics? Is he still a revisionist?'

'He's still a member of the Communist Party. Keeps him busy with meetings, committees.'

'Traitors.' Her left hand tightened into a fist, hitting the marble tabletop with a barely audible thump. 'With their historical compromise. Damned traitors, all of them.' Her fingers unfurled and lay, still tight with tension, white against the black marble. Those long cool fingers around his throat.

With his sister, a visiting cousin, and Antonio from the neighbouring *palazzo* he and Elena were playing 'murder' in the Morosini's private apartments. It was a dark winter afternoon. The Morosinis were away at one of their other houses in Milan or Rome. White dust covers were spread over the plush sofas, the antique sideboards and tables. The slips of paper were drawn, the heavy satin drapes pulled, the light from the ornate Murano chandelier switched off. Disappointed at drawing neither detective nor murderer and thus consigned to victimhood, he moved away from the others. He retreated beneath the side table with the Roman bust. Through the dust cover he could hear muffled giggles, the odd thud or exclamation. But he was separate, on some other level of existence, isolated with the dry taste of dust, the mothball-scented sheets, the impenetrable blackness.

The pictures began to form on his eyelids. But while they were still shadows, on the edge of his mind, while his stomach still contracted in apprehension at what it knew was to come, he shoved the sheet aside. He crawled along the edge of the Persian rug, only standing when he reached the door to the balcony. He tried to control his breathing but it was embarrassingly loud and fast. Searching for air, he stepped out. As he stood in the icy dampness, breathing hard, he noticed for the first time the small stone lions perched on the filigreed railing, noticed, in particular, the one lion that faced in, rather than out. He ran his fingers over the worn stone. The lion had been carved out of the same pillar that formed the corner column and could not be removed without marring the whole balcony. The unknown medieval artist had been careful to make his act of rebellion permanent.

And it was there that Elena found him, that she wrapped her long, cool fingers around his throat, wrenching him out of his concentration on the grey sky, the mournful, static canal. Her body pressed against his, pelvis to buttocks, the softness of her just-formed breasts caressing his back. 'Murder' — and when he didn't fall to the floor as expected, whispering in his ear: 'You're dead, silly' — her fingers tightening on his throat. The scent from her hair and mouth and skin everywhere. He turned quickly, to prolong this new delight, grasping her with both hands, managing a kiss only slightly to the side of her opened mouth. Those long fingers still around his aching throat, the nails pressing. 'I said, murder.'

His hand was covering hers. She stopped in mid-sentence, staring down, forgetting momentarily the perfidy of Berlinguer.

'Do you remember when we were children together? Playing at the Morosini's? Remember?'

She beamed her clear, blue eyes on him, leaving her hand cool under his. 'Where are the days of yesteryear? And all that? Nostalgia is a trap, Marco. There were no golden days.'

He withdrew his hand, pushed back his chair, and reached for his coat.

'No, no. Don't go. We never see each other. Look, you're still damp. Come on. Sit down again. There's so much you haven't told me about. It's always awkward at first, after so long.' It was the old, warm face glowing at him now. Her voice was deep and rich like melted caramel. 'And your family? Paola?'

'She got promoted at work. She's a supervisor now.'

'But between you and me, it's not good? Don't look surprised. Your mother and mine still talk, you know.'

'Well, you know what mothers are like.'

'Seriously, it isn't going well, is it?'

'Paola has a lot of strain on her with Francesco and all.'

'Is it just that?'

'Just? You try it.'

'Look, I'm sorry, really,' her voice pouring over him. 'But I do understand.' She paused to light a cigarette.

'You are no longer with Giorgio?'

'Two years now. We've filed for divorce.'

'Now I'm sorry.'

'Why? You wouldn't believe how much better it is for me. I married for the wrong reason, just as I think you did. Stop bristling.' She laid her hand with the burning cigarette on his arm. 'We both married symbols of what we wanted. I thought I was marrying a proletarian comrade.'

'His factory murals are very good. Quite first class.'

'Yes, he has the luxury of feeling himself allied to the working class while remaining comfortably petty bourgeois. It was appealing, very appealing, but I finally had to face the inauthenticity.' She shot one of her smiles at the waiter bringing the new espressos she had ordered. 'And you, you wanted to move up in class, and Paola — oh, she was so much the bourgeois, complete with all the benefits, the house, the friends, etc.'

He protested: 'You reduce. My family isn't exactly working.'

'No, not quite, failed aristocrats, but failed generations ago. Long enough that the only significance is pride.'

42

He swallowed his coffee in one gulp. 'You have the system — so everything fits, neatly. But it isn't that simple. Or easy. I mean what about Francesco? How will he be "solved" after the revolution? Or won't there be any Francescos? Will you rid yourselves of all defectives?'

She was shaking her head. 'You've lost all perspective. You've allowed your personal pain to —'

'There's always personal pain. You can't abolish that.'

'But there can be support, help. For example, if there were institutions — wait — not like the ones we have today but proper places with trained personnel.'

Crossing his legs to the side, turning his body and head away from her, the doorway came into his line of vision. A tall, heavily made-up woman with sausage curls, lacquered in place all over her head, was entering. Adolfo was behind her, his grey head peeking over her shoulder. 'Christ.' Adolfo had obviously caught sight of him and Elena; he was grinning, exposing his teeth. 'Now he'll think . . . Just what he would like to think too.' Lifting his arm and flashing Marco the circular 'all right' sign, Adolfo and the woman crossed over to the bar.

'Who on earth is he? And that woman? It's a miracle that she hasn't been washed away on a night like tonight.'

Marco told her in a low voice. While Adolfo

kept sending them smiles across the room, he described the scene in the office and the new project for the Lido. Elena responded, as expected, with the political line of 'What can you expect?' and 'Venice is dying. There's no hope for her anyway.' But their common outrage relaxed them, bringing them closer to each other.

'Look, the rain has stopped. I really must go.'

'Sorry you ran into me?' Her eyes, clear and blue.

'Of course not.'

'Even though I harassed you?'

'I was happy to see you. Honestly. But I must go.'

'Yes, Paola must be wondering.' So he explained that she was in Padova with Francesco for tests, that he was expected at Tarquinio's. As he spoke, Marco was standing, leaning over the table. Suddenly her long, cool fingers covered his fist still resting on the marble. 'So you'll be alone tonight.'

'Alone with my thoughts.'

Her eyes grew more intense than they had yet been, as if she was taking his measure. 'Till later then.'

Conceding only a short nod to Adolfo and his friend as he passed, Marco walked out of the café and into the wet night, wondering whether he was expected to read another level into her polite phrase.

IV

He was aware of his legs and pleased by that, for him, unusual awareness of movement, strength, capability. He carried with it a concrete sense of Elena's body and a score of newly-minted fantasies. His hands on her fuzzy blonde head, her mouth and tongue paying tribute to his flesh. More theatrically, he saw her bound and gagged, a bit afraid, waiting.

Across the empty square of Campo Bartolomeo, the light glinted on the centre statue, the wet pavement stones, so he felt as if he had stumbled upon a stage. The audience watching him from behind the shuttered windows. Both he and they waiting for the action to begin.

He broke into a slight run. *Calle*. Bridge. One more — the last narrow street was blocked off. The police stood in silence, one at each end, the rest towards the middle in a cluster, staring up at one of the upper floors. Silent. Uncertain or expectant? Their white diagonal sashes and white gloves aggressive in the darkness.

His hurried footsteps sounded unusually guilty, melodramatic, so that it was with a certain relief that he reached his brother's building.

Marco had barely begun the stairs when the door to Tarquinio's third floor apartment was thrown open, the light cutting the stairwell's darkness, illuminating the damp stains, the patches of crumbling plaster, the scent of onion and frying fish managing to overpower the stale urine and rot. Barbara stood in the light, hopping on one leg in excitement. 'But where have you been? Paola phoned and you weren't here. She was mad. Wouldn't talk to anyone else. She could have said something to us, but . . .' The contrast between her lovely little, grey-eyed face, sing-songish child's voice and the familiar nagging adult tone of the words was startling. 'Of course, she wouldn't. Oh, you're all wet!'

He heard the same and more in the kitchen. His mother and aunt swept around him, divesting him of his wet clothes, pushing cups of warm tea. Clucking. Clucking.

'Enough!' Marco pushed aside the cup his mother held up to his lips. 'Why don't we sit down and start eating so you can all stop complaining.'

'Actually,' Barbara had managed to stick close to him, 'we started already. We ate the pasta.'

'So you aren't exactly starving.'

His aunt Elsa, less than five feet tall but imposing in her stockiness, put on her official disapproving face. 'We waited an hour, but since you didn't have the courtesy to even phone . . .'

'I could have been earlier and wetter, or later and drier. I chose the path of compromise and managed, as usual, to displease everyone.' Managing in fact to deflect his mother from starting a no doubt long argument with her sister and managing to get everyone to laugh.

Marco watched them sink back into their meal. Tarquinio ate methodically — first the veal, then the peas then the salad; his face, a slightly more refined version of Marco's own, giving his plate the same expression (concern with a touch of detached amusement) that it wore in dealing with his family. Barbara pushed bits of meat around her plate, looking up only to make faces of complicity at Marco. Lea, tiny and dark, was in the midst of an argument with Patrizia, the older child. Her head shot forward to meet her fork and her mouth grasped the food in a short, fast gobble. 'If you realized how silly you looked with all that goop on your face.'

Patrizia, meanwhile, was eating in an exaggeratedly polite way, managing to lay the food in her mouth without disturbing her red painted lips. 'The trouble with you, Mother, is that you're jealous.' Such slow, slow chews. 'You want to keep me a child forever.'

'The trouble with adolescents,' Tarquinio commented *sotto voce* to Marco, 'is that they're so predictable. Boringly so. Never seem to say anything new.'

Their mother and Aunt Elsa sat, with matching faces and jaw movements, at the end of the table closest to the kitchen. Both had trouble with their false teeth, but Aunt Elsa, a spinster and more susceptible to the rules of gentility, made more of an effort to eat with her mouth closed and not to fish out tough bits with her fingers. 'It is true, Lea, that these days all the girls — and I'm talking about the well-bred ones too — the ones from nice families — make themselves up.'

Her sister's mouth widened in protest, almost losing some of its contents. 'Don't be stupid, Elsa. If the other girls throw themselves into the canal does that mean Patrizia should?'

Marco sipped at the mineral water, the icy bubbles clearing away the bad taste.

'Marco. You haven't eaten anything!' A casual glance down the table had changed his mother's focus of interest. 'You can't go on like this. You must eat.'

'He ate a bit of bread.' Barbara volunteered, in an effort to be helpful.

'But try. A few peas.'

'What about mothers?' Marco aimed at Tarquinio. 'Are they ever original?'

His brother laughed. 'I suppose when we play our roles, we're all predictable.'

'And when do we ever step out?' But before Tarquinio could answer, their mother had left her chair and was bearing down on them. Like her sister, she was short, though thin. But, despite her stick-like arms and legs, her body, with its fallen breasts and inflated stomach, had presence. She leaned over Marco's shoulder cajoling, rearranging the food on his plate with his fork, offering to heat up the leftover pasta.

'Mamma. Please.' He saw Tarquinio and Lea exchange one of their knowing glances.

'Can't you understand why I'd be nervous tonight of all nights? Waiting for Paola's call? If I knew how Francesco was.'

His mother drew back, her large, knuckled hand dropping to his shoulder. 'Yes. Of course. I wonder why she isn't calling. It's been a while now.'

'It's like her. To make me wait. Knowing how anxious I'd be.' Lea's dark gaze flickered for a moment and she drew up ever so slightly, signaling to Marco she thought this remark was the wrong note, inappropriate. Trying to change the topic (his mother was sitting down again, but her eyes had that glassy glow that precedes a teary outburst), 'I ran into Elena on my way home.'

'Elena!' A universal chorus.

'She didn't look too bad. She said she's divorced.'

'You see,' his mother was tearing a crusty roll to bits. 'Her mother always insists that she's still married. Says he's away working. Won't admit a thing.'

'She's from the South, isn't she?'

'She's been here fifty years.'

'Oh, those people . . .'

'Did she seem happy?' Tarquinio didn't look at Marco but into his wine glass as he asked.

'Funny, she was interested in knowing how you were . . .'

Patrizia raised her voice, cutting in. 'I told you I saw her last year. When there was that strike at school.'

'Dear God. A strike at school. What days we're living in.'

'You didn't tell me.' Elsa's voice was resigned.

'Yes, I did. During the sit-in. Remember the *Indiani metropolitani* turned up?'

'Elena was decked out in paints and feathers — dancing?' Lea giggled.

'Nooo. She just turned up and watched without saying anything. Smiled a few times. It was spooky. I know I told you.'

The two older women drew on all their indignation and began on the weakness of the modern school system, the ingratitude of the students, the horror of all demonstrations and disruptions.

'Actually, Elena said she'd given up on all that,' Marco interjected in another attempt to calm everyone.

'Did you hear there was a hold-up today at

the Banca di Roma near the *Piazzale*?' Lea offered.

'A hold-up? In Venice? I've never heard of such a thing.'

'Dear God.'

'Political?'

'I don't know. All I heard was there were two armed men. It was just before lunch so there were hundreds of people about. But they still got away. Walked right out and over the bridge. They must have had a car waiting at the *Piazzale*.'

'But no one was hurt?'

'Of course. No one was killed, but one of the guards was shot and a customer — a mother with three children.'

'Dear God. Dear, dear God.'

'None of us is safe these days. None of us.'

'And they think one of the thieves . . .'

They all spoke louder and louder, their words fueled by boundless anger, their faces animated, almost happy.

'Come on,' Tarquinio leaned towards his brother. 'Off to the living room. Bianca just sent me a collection of The Platters' *Greatest Hits*. You need it tonight. I need it tonight.'

The smooth, creamy music filled the room, sealing off the door, cutting off the voices from the kitchen. It was a room that bore Tarquinio's imprint more strongly than any other in the apartment. The furniture was modern — steel, glass, and leather — reflecting the formal, rigorous side of Tarquinio's nature, his desire that everything be exactly right. The books were nineteenth-century classics mixed with works of Marxist theory. The paintings were mostly his own — large, brightly-coloured impressions of Venice — interspersed with a few cubist prints.

'*Adrift in a world of my own.*' Tarquinio stood smoking, an elbow on the bookcase. 'Have you ever listened to the words?'

'Pardon?' Marco had sunk into the sofa.

'I never tried to understand the words before. Strange. After twenty years of hearing a song, but I finally listened. Adrift in a world of my own.' He translated, '*Alla deriva nel mio mondo.*'

But his brother only smiled. 'Well, if you're going to get all serious, why not Battista? Or Bennato, or Dylan, if you're going to play the American?'

'No, they don't have the same meaning for me. They can't. The Platters, the Inkspots: that was music.'

'There is an age difference between us. Still I understand. First fuck. Elena was telling me today about the dangers of nostalgia.'

'Speaking of nostalgia.'

'I bet.'

'Not that way. We started on Marx together.'

'The way I remember it, it was she and I that began reading together.'

'You're wrong, little brother. It was Elena and I. Our minds in a mutual, intellectual first flowering. What shoots! What buds!'

'I told her you were happy . . . she was skeptical.'

Tarquinio butted his cigarette and dropped onto the sofa. 'Too real is the feeling of make-believe. Woo-oooh. Ah yes. I suppose I am — resigned if nothing else. Before I was married, I was desperate to leave Venice — to leave Italy. I felt if I could just get away from the family, the class system, the useless, endless politics, the rot.'

Marco was pleased that Tarquinio was speaking in such a way to him. If he was asked he would say that he and his brother were close, that they understood each other. But the understanding couldn't come from the words they exchanged, for generally they spoke only of the details of their lives. It came from their tone, the matching irony. 'And you tried?'

Tarquinio seemed about to go on, beyond anecdote, but just as he began to speak, their mother, tray in hand, appeared at the door. He fell back into his usual style. 'As they say in America, three strikes and you're out.'

'You must have wondered what happened to me. Turn that down.' She bustled over to the coffee table. 'But the kitchen was in such a mess.' She glanced over at Tarquinio to see if her barb at Lea had taken. 'So loud you have to have that record?'

Down the hall, the phone rang, slicing the oohs and aahs from the stereo, freezing all three of them: she bent over the cups, spoons in hand, Tarquinio cigarette extended, Marco running his fingers through his tight curls. But the name Barbara called out was Patrizia. Their mother went back to stirring the sugar into the coffee. 'That girl spends all her time on the phone. Milk, Marco?'

'No. Thank you.'

'But why not? It's good for you. Nutritious.'

'A spoonful of milk?'

'Better than nothing.'

'Mother, you know I never take milk in coffee. Why every time, we have to . . .' But the protest was a token one since she had poured the milk in before she had asked if he wanted any.

Tarquinio, grimacing lit yet another cigarette. 'Mamma, he's no longer a little boy. He can take care of himself. The way you treat him, it's no wonder.'

Their mother arranged her face in an innocent expression as she headed for the door. 'He can? Really?'

The record ended, the needle clicking as it hit the centre over and over. Marco waited for his brother to explain, but Tarquinio continued to stare at the bottom of his coffee cup. Finally he laid the black porcelain cup back on the saucer and got up to flip over the record. 'But I have said it all before.'

'What? About emigration?'

'About you.' Marco felt as if he had been born without skin so that all his insides were visible. His brother's words floating out of his mouth across the room, landed on his vulnerable flesh with a sting.

'Not tonight, brother.'

'Laughing friends denyyiiii.' Tarquinio turned full-face to Marco. 'But I think it would do you good for us to discuss it.'

'Not tonight.' He was firm. 'Back to emigration.'

'You've heard all my stories.' While still a teenager, Tarquinio had gone to Canada. After two years he had come back with tales of the intolerable cold and of the ugliness of both country and people. Later, he had tried London, and it was there that he had met Lea, who had been visiting her estranged father. On each of their holidays for eight years, Tarquinio would be brimming with fresh examples of rudeness and prejudice. (Dramatic scenes of Tarquinio confronting various English bosses over ill-chosen words. All to prove to them that Italians were not the nothings they thought.) He wouldn't have left a third time, but the shipyard he worked in lost too many contracts. After months without work, he had left alone for Switzerland. Six months of isolation, six months of truly being seen as nothing. 'Probably you would have done it better. Been more successful.'

'Why? Because I'm not so quick-tempered. You think I'm placid?'

Tarquinio shrugged his shoulders. 'My name was my doom. I would have made a good Etruscan warrior.'

'Defending your city to the death.'

'Umm. Which brings us to why you never went. You would never leave Venice.'

'Can't imagine it. Safe harbour and all that.'

'What I hated was that I was never in context. I mean, at first I'd stand back and criticize.'

'I remember.'

'Yes, but eventually I'd understand that I wasn't seeing the place at all. The longer I stayed the more I realized how little I comprehended. I felt I could only take part on a very superficial level. Maybe if I . . .'

The phone again. Marco leapt up but stopped himself from running into the hall. Finally, 'Marco. It's Paola.'

'I was waiting.'

'I called before, but you weren't there. Her voice was neutral, matter-of-fact.

'He's all right? I mean he got through?'

'Obviously. Don't you think you would have heard?'

'Was he frightened?' The cold-eyed, masked men.

'Look, I don't want to go into details over the phone. When I get home.'

'10:15 at the *Piazzale*.'

'No, it's going to be later. Probably in the evening. There has to be another consultation.'

'Why? What does Lambrusco say?'

'He won't tell me anything yet. You know what doctors are like. He did say it was serious. Very serious. But we knew that.'

'But Francesco . . .' Invaded to the core of his helpless self.

'I told you. He's all right. He's asleep; they gave him a shot.'

'You didn't tell me.'

They went on: she explaining her arrangements, how she could be reached. 'I should have been with you. If I had known it was going to be two days. I didn't realize.'

'I'm managing.' Probably better without him and his anxiety.

'Of course. But I'm still concerned about you.'

'Well, naturally I was tense.'

'Try to get some sleep tonight. Did you remember to take your pills with you?' And he did wish he was with her. That he could hold her with gentleness and support. 'I miss you both.' She didn't reply to his unusual endearment. 'I do.'

He thought he'd report to the kitchen and the living room as quickly as he could. He needed to be alone to draw inward, to examine and place the variety of feelings that fought to overwhelm him. They all complained, of course, that he had barely got there, that there hadn't been time to visit, that he shouldn't go off and brood. But he held out.

At the door, while his mother was helping him on with his coat, rambling on about the cold and the wet, Barbara suddenly appeared and attached herself to his waist.

'Is Francesco OK?'

Marco explained again.

'Can I come and see him on Sunday? I'll bring him a present and play with him.' Her little face was sober. 'I can make him feel better.' She rarely asked to visit her cousin and, in fact, Paola discouraged children from visiting out of fear that they might be harbouring germs or viruses. But when Barbara did see Francesco she always treated him with the same serious, almost reverent manner.

'That's very nice of you. He'd love it.'

Barbara let go of his waist and took a step back. 'Uncle, I think sometimes you forget that Francesco is magical.' Closing her grey eyes to emphasize her point, 'He has smiles in his fingertips.'

V

The piercing light of the low midday sun pours through the two high windows, lays stripes of blinding brightness across the carpets, the walls, the desk, and the pile of ink-covered papers. I wish I could make you see this book-stuffed room where I sit and write. Make you know me as I know you: know your study, the drafting tables, the discreet bed-sofa, the ordered shelves, the blown-up pictures of the lagoon; know your light: never this direct, cheerful shine but always a reflection flickering up from the canal, a watery, shifting glow that plays over the pictures, the fading gold and brown ceiling frescoes. Make you know me as I know you: as I have always known you. For you are within me, the emblem of my inner city.

As I look over those three earlier novels, I see that my changing needs, my shifting perceptions and understanding, cast you in different forms, bestowing different roles, different masks. Would you recognize yourself, acknowledge that those eyes the masks couldn't cover were your eyes? This time I am below the masks. As my need has shrunk, my narration has drawn closer. And this time, I am within you, within the city of my mind, that mirage on the horizon, that stone reality, that maze of curving streets that draws me deeper and deeper. My outer city, Edmonton, draws never in but out to immensity, to limitlessness, to the indifference of land not yet shaped by man's hand.

I live alone now, alone except for my two cats Paolo and Sarpi, in a small house in one of the relatively older treed areas of this still-infant city. One or two lifetimes ago all this, besides a tiny garrison, was wilderness; the ever-spreading grid of streets and buildings must have been unimaginable. And still, that sense of the wild, the oceans of untouched plains, forests, and tundra is there, above and beneath the skyscrapers and traffic jams. For the city is still not fully imagined. It seems precarious, even transitory, an imposition rather than a natural growth, a partnership of man and the elements. So many are here to take what they can. When the boom slackens, when the flow of money and oil is cut, they will pack up their buildings and move on to a new camp. Yet, I feel comfortable, at home in the deepest sense: my house, my city. Partly because that sense of the wild has become necessary to me. Just five houses away, at the end of the block, there is a deep ravine with a creek at the bottom that curves its way to the river valley. So even though I live close to the central core of glass and cement skyscrapers, even though when I sit in my backyard on a summer evening I can hear the roar of trucks on the nearby thoroughfare and almost smell the noxious fumes, in a minute I can lose myself to the ravine woods where the only sound is that of running water and of birds and squirrels in the trees, where the only smell is the scent of pine or wildflowers.

It was Jack who taught me the names of the flowers — Indian paintbrush, Queen Anne's lace, fairy bells, who taught me to recognize the different species of mushrooms, to categorize the different types of birch. He insisted I learn how to cross-country ski. Remembering my childhood struggle to learn how to skate, remembering the sore ankles and the many hard falls, I was convinced I couldn't do it. But Jack was not easily deterred and I found I could. Gliding through the white, tree-bordered fields, gliding through the silence, the cold air not a blow but a caress on my overheated cheeks. In the summer and fall, long walks along the winding river and expeditions to the country to visit the last ferry that crossed the North Saskatchewan River, the graveyard at Pakan, the church at Frog Lake. And, always, the pauses, the halts for my instruction. Note well this bird, that flower. Irritating sometimes but, as you know, I have always had a weakness for the man who aims to teach me. I am both practical and lazy. I take pleasure from just knowing, no matter how random, how disconnected the item of information. And the easiest way of assimilation is through the medium of an interesting man, particularly one who has worked out his system of connections, of eliminating the seeming randomness. I crave patterns; I am drawn to concerned stances, not to adopt but to test.

I have always thought that words were a medium. One understands, one thinks, one expresses this through and by language. But I have very little interest in language as simply language. If words for me are at all things, they are things to be wrestled with, to be forced into the proper order so that they approximate what I am interested in expressing. But for Jack, words, in whatever language, were primarily objects to be inspected and reverently wondered over. 'City,' he would say,'from the Latin *civis* and *civitas,* the place where the citizen is at home. Are you at home?' he would tease, 'a citizen? We could make Edmonton a city. We citizens could make it.'

Or once, 'What do you call this?' he asked in mock innocence, pointing with a spatula to the pan where he was cooking an omelet.

'Fry pan,' I replied absently.

'Aaahh.' He was triumphant. 'Fry pan. You are an Albertan. Your words give you away.'

'Don't be silly. It was a slip. I usually say frying pan,' knowing I didn't.

'You say *fry pan*,' gloating almost, as if he'd found a ten dollar bill in the gutter.

'Pedant. Stop analysing me. It's for me to decide what I am.'

Yet in teaching me to recognize, teaching me to name, he changed me. It was as if the emotional slide through which I had been viewing the land, the slide that coloured the country oppressive and infinitely barren, flipped up and back to be stored; a new one that painted the land familiar and supporting clicked into place.

Old masks replaced by new? The vision of the outsider, Italian, American, or Eastern Canadian, superseded by that of the native? Partly. I did take on an attitude that was not only Jack's, but, with variations, that of his friends; an attitude of almost self-conscious concern, though still, at the base, an attitude of true interest. There were two poets, a folk singer, a quilt maker, various teachers and journalists, and several would-be film makers and artists in Jack's group. They were as different from each other as members of a group can be, but they all shared a sense of their own strength and of their own capability.

But I felt, I still feel, that I was doing more than simply absorbing their views, their masks. I was looking through. I was finally seeing what was here because I had finally lost my expectations of what should be here.

You, of course, met Jack, hosted him in

your home, but much of him would remain hidden in a habitat so different from his natural one. I imagined, even without Aunt Elsa's comments, how odd he must have seemed with his long hair and beard, his faded clothes, just the sheer height and weight of him. And what he would be interested in seeing in Venice would seem deliberately eccentric: the Greek Orthodox Church, the Armenian island, the new ghetto. Certainly Jack was not above setting himself noticeably apart from the usual tourist pack, not above emphasizing his original taste; but he would know that in Venice no choices are individual and that his were, after all, for a man of Ukrainian ancestry, almost routine. Still, you liked him, your mother liked him, even Aunt Elsa approved. His energy and enthusiasm came through despite the filter of his hesitant, limited Italian. And perhaps it was the limits of his Italian that led him to declare us engaged. I should have presumed it was a simple mistake. At the time, however, I did not receive your congratulations graciously. It seemed a perfect example of his high-handedness. We had once played at being engaged, played with the idea of marriage. It is difficult not to act out the assigned roles: the man and woman meet, they make love, they move in together, they discover indeed they are in love. Therefore, he must be the much-awaited prince, she the lovely princess. There must be a happily-ever-after, a validation. Our mock engagement occurred on a day in early spring. We were driving out to a lake for the first picnic of the year. We were already off the highway, barrelling along the gravel road when Jack turned the Volkswagen down a narrow, puddle-filled path; then again through a gap in a fence to the centre of a field where, as soon as the wheels stopped turning, the car sank into the gumbo. 'What are you doing? Why on earth did we stop here?' I had opened the door and was perched on the running board. The field stretched over the top of a gentle hill so that from our spot in the centre, one could see for miles: gentle curves marked with patches of poplar and pine, mounds of snow, the wet, dark earth.

'You aren't thinking here, in the open?'

Jack, smiling the mock-naive smile he reserved for such times, was leaning out from the driver's seat, over my place, his hand stretched out, inching its way up my thigh.

'Jack. Don't . . .' His caress turned to a pull, tumbling me back into the car.

After the harshness of the just-departed winter, the heat of the sun on our naked skin was an intoxicating rediscovery. My belly, his buttocks, were dazzlingly white, not with the dead white of snow but with the glowing cleanness of life. Through the open doors came the stink of a Western spring. The snow was in retreat, exposing last year's vegetation, last year's garbage. Still, underneath the rot, there was a bracing tang, not yet a new beginning but the potential, the ready fertility of that earth. Afterwards, naturally, the car wouldn't budge. I took Jack's place in the driver's seat and he positioned himself behind to push. We moved out of the field slowly, with sudden bursts forward and sudden stalls. By the time we reached the opening in the fence the bottom half of his legs and arms was covered with the heavy, clinging mud.

'Wipe it off,' I insisted as he tried to reclaim his seat. 'You can't get in like that.'

'Why ever not?' Those encrusted hands were on my pale pink blouse, lifting me out by the rib cage. Naturally I yelled, but the yells, as Jack's intention of removing me from the driver's seat turned to a more devilish purpose, flowed into giggles.

'I' the mire. I' the mire.' Jack was both pulling and stroking. 'How about trying the hood?'

So we did. Exposed to the road, the field. Mud, grit, metal against my slightly twisted back. Still, I was weightless. I soared, flew up into that limitless, absolute sky.

At the lake itself, we walked once up and down the wet beach. The cabins bordering the beach were still boarded up, the lake still frozen. As we started back to the car, Jack stopped suddenly and bent to the dark sand. He was almost smiling, a slight twist of the mouth, but his movements were formal. He lifted my hand. 'Bianca, wilt thou be my wife?'

pushing over my finger the pop-can ring he'd found.

'Of course . . . of course.' I adjusted the metal circle as carefully as if it were a priceless diamond. 'Forever.' We exchanged the usual words, lines from pop songs. Maybe I did believe them, maybe he did, but it was too theatrical: the acting out of storybooks. Why couldn't he see that? I knew as soon as he left the city to begin his European trek that he and I were too exotic for each other, too much an exciting vacation, too little the solidity of home. Jack felt we could construct that stable base, but out of his bricks. The instruction would be stepped up. I refused to learn the Cyrillic alphabet. Undaunted, he pasted labels with the appropriate Ukrainian names, translit-erated, on all the household objects. Mirror, *dzerkalo*, bed, *lizhko*, table, *stil*. Mirror, my face pale and long, bed, Jack stretched out, beautiful. Embroidered runners on the furni-ture, folkloric candlesticks, reproduction ikons. 'The expression of the people,' he would say, 'for there were no Ukrainian bourgeois, you know,' and let himself go, drifting off on a his-torical lecture.

We drifted on — until a Sunday after Easter. We were at a special prayer service at a church in the small town of Smoky Lake, where Jack's grandparents were buried. The ceremony went on and on. First there were prayers in the church, a procession out to a series of tables bearing *Pomana*, commemorative Easter breads, and *pomenyk*, family death books. The priest blessed the bread, the books. Then, he went on to read the list of names in each black book. His voice, the warm, spring sun, the weight of the commemoration beat at me. I should not have been there. It was not my place. When the priest began the blessing of the graves, I pulled at Jack's arm. 'I've got to go. We've got to go.'

'Not too much longer, sweetie. When he passes the family's grave, we can sit and eat.'

'I don't want to eat on a grave.' I could no longer whisper.'I feel faint. Weighed down . . . I can't breathe. *Please*.'

He came with me, but his eyes, the set of his mouth, were resentful, suspicious.

He was so good at getting his way. His strength of will matched the strength of his big, muscular body. But I could not give myself up totally. I could not be joined to him by words in an alien tongue, tied by unknown gestures and ritual cloths. I let myself be changed, not remade. And as I pulled back and resisted, he happened upon someone more malleable, not 'Engleesh' as his relatives labelled me, no matter how I protested.

Now I am alone. I tease myself with fantasies. You calling from the airport. 'Pick me up. I'm here.'

You could hide out in this house. I could put on the nurturing role. Hold your hand as you talked, iron your shirt, tempt you back to food with homemade pasta so light and desserts so sweet that eating them would be a long interior caress. I could soothe. I could heal. If only I had the chance.

Fantasies. You will never come. Instead there is talk of sending Barbara. Lea writes that the child needs a change, needs a place where 'nothing happens', where she can go freely to the corner store, to school, where she can lose her fear.

I am alone. I sit in my study and stare out the high windows at the bare, grey boughs, or I stand by my front window fixed on a dusty street, empty, except for the occasional jogger, the odd car. I am motionless, waiting for the long blight of winter to begin.

Winter, no longer just the long blight. Winter, my country. Snow, my country. I am no longer afraid of the vastness, the extremity of this place. Yet even as I stare out the window, the labyrinthine *calle* of Venice are close, so very close, inevitably drawing me. I hear the noisy cheerful sound of the Venetian crowd on the main paths, the silent darkness of the back ways. I see the canals, the shops, the squares as you pass. The news vendor on the corner, at the end of your road, the main door to your apartment building. I see each room, each corner. I see Elena as she slips in the door. I see the avidness with which you pull her to you, with which you incline your face to hers.

The hunger in your mouth the second before it takes hers. And I smell not her perfume but yours. Clean, metallic, male, with a touch of sweet sweat, it engulfs me as completely as if it rose from my own cold pores.

Night

VI

Almost without thinking, Marco did what he would always do when he came home late in the evening, he went straight to Francesco's room. He would open the door very slowly, so it wouldn't creak, pick his way around the toys scattered around the room, until he stood by the bed. Francesco's fat little body sprawled in sleep looked almost normal, and it was in these quiet moments that Marco felt the clearest, the most uncomplicated tenderness for his son.

But, of course, tonight the bed was empty. Marco sat down, turning on the plastic bear sidelight. The room was permeated with Francesco's smell — a combination of urine, essence of wild violets that Paola insisted on rubbing into his hair ('it covers up a bit'), and the sour tang of his flesh. Marco breathed deeply, drawing it in, as if he were drinking a long, cold drink on a hot day.

He always remembered the first time they saw Francesco in washed-out colours, as if his memory had used overexposed film. The white canvas curtain separating them from the rest of the chattering ward. Paola's pale, pale face against the pillow. His wrinkly, large-knuckled hand on the edge of the bed. Only the bouquet of overblown roses on the side-table seemed real in their deep, velvety redness. The white-coated doctor, after many emotionless medical words, stood aside to let the nursing sister wheel the bassinet up to the bed. Paola leaned forward, her face almost eager, but just as her hand touched the edge of the blue blanket, her face twisted, as if about to crack. 'He was supposed to be perfect. I was sure.' She turned her face away to the roses. 'Not yet.'

So Marco had held him first, held that bundle of living, breathing child. And, with the tenderness, he felt exposed, flayed alive. 'Pray. That's the only thing we can do for Francesco,' his mother had said when Marco had gone to the kitchen to report on Paola's call. 'I lit some candles today at *La Madonna della Salute*, but tomorrow I'll go again. The Virgin won't let us down.'

Marco had shrugged his shoulders, irritated but not wanting to begin another argument. His mother misread the shrug. 'I know.' Her voice was unusually soft. 'Sometimes I think it would be better if he died. You can't carry this burden on and on.'

His rage had been instantaneous, total. Sitting on his son's bed, staring at the bright alphabet and number poster he and Paola had hung in such hope before Francesco's birth, Marco wondered at that rage. It was such an overreaction to what was a well-meant comment. Why couldn't he have simply answered that it would not be better; that he never never wished such for his son.

For six long years he had been willing Francesco life. Six long, long years of waiting and working — each normal step of development stretched out. One year before Francesco could turn over. Two years before he could sit up. Four before he took his first step. Each level of mundane mechanics became an achievement, more a victory. The six longest years of Marco's life. But his will for his son had never wavered, not once.

Marco stretched out his hand to touch the large holy medallion his mother had insisted on attaching to the headboard of Francesco's bed. It consisted of a child Jesus beaten out of silver against a gold-coloured background. The crown, sceptre, and robes were impressively ornate and detailed while the face was totally human, cheerful, even a touch mischievous. 'If we just pray enough,' his mother would say, 'the solution will come. Your grandmother always said, "God closes a door but he opens a window."' And (poor woman) she had certainly tried to pray enough, a multitude of hours on her knees in various churches around the city, before various noted statues and paintings. She had a legalistic view of the relation between God and man. A person prayed and God, somehow, would answer. A person lived according to the laws of God and man, and he was owed some luck and some fortune. When Marco pointed out exceptions to her theory, good people struck down for no apparent reason, she would only shake her head and declare, 'You don't know what was in their hearts. God knows who to reward and who to punish.' And when he pressed further, calling her faith mere superstition, she had answered him with, 'If you only had had faith, if only you had gone to mass — at least during the pregnancy.' Marco suddenly wondered what she could have been praying *for* over the past years. Certainly not for Francesco's cure. He could only be what he was. Even she couldn't believe in that kind of miracle. For his death then? So her comment that evening had not been casual; she had always wished it.

His rage was there again — instantly. Like a machine. Certain subjects brought certain responses. 'Resignation,' the nun on the baby ward, her little yellow face screwed up in its earnestness, had suggested. 'You must resign yourself to God's will. We all have our personal crosses to bear.'

'Patience,' Padre Lino, the priest who had blessed them with the sacrament of matrimony, had counselled. 'Love. Kindness. But in return who knows how much joy? How many blessings? We cannot know God's plan.'

But his patience, his resignation could only be superficial, because in his centre he was sure there was no Will, no Plan. There was no meaning to Francesco, especially not that of personal burden, personal punishment.

Surprisingly, ominously, the phone began to ring. Marco ran out of the room, down the hall, picking up the receiver before the third ring. But, on the other end, there was only silence. Then a click. Machine-man Marco. Smiling slightly, he turned into his bedroom. He took out from his coat pocket the box with the ring he had brought Paola. He hung his coat in the closet and hid the box in his underwear drawer. It was good that he hadn't mentioned the ring at Tarquinio's. To go into debt for a birthday present — that would have brought out the brotherly and motherly sage advice. The act would seem excessive to all of them, even Lea. Only Marco knew how necessary the excessive and extravagant gift was for him and Paola. He went back down the hall to the blue and white tile kitchen for his nightly cup of camomile tea. Paola had left everything ready. The kettle was on the stove. The box of tea bags, the teapot, cup and saucer, jar of honey and sliced lemon were arranged neatly under a large linen napkin. She'd even laid out two digestive biscuits on the edge of the saucer. She catered to his stomach although she couldn't quite believe there was anything wrong with it. 'Your mother just spoiled you,' she announced after they were married, when he refused a dish she had spent an hour preparing. 'Separate menus. None of this. None of that. It's all in your head. That's where your pain is.'

'I only wish it was. You know very well they took out my stomach. You can't expect me to be ordinary . . .'

'You're exaggerating. If you could only be more sensible.'

'If you could only understand.'

Still, if she were with him now he could have told her about his feelings in Francesco's room. In that place she was equally vulnerable.

He poured the clear yellow tea from pot to cup; he stirred the honey in slowly, intent on the ripples and the delicate, faint scent so evocative of summer fields.

The doorbell rang, louder than the telephone. He played at imagining his mother stopping by on her way home or a neighbour wanting news of Francesco. It was only about 10:30. But he knew who it was. Had he not been waiting, anticipating, all evening?

Elena looked so different standing in the darkened hall that, for a second, he thought he had been wrong. Her hair was no longer frizzy but straight, long and thick. Her formerly bare face was brightly painted and her neutral clothes replaced by tight and garish ones. 'Are you alone?' she whispered.

'I said I would be.'

She pushed past him into the apartment. 'Before someone sees me.' When he turned back to her after relocking the door, she was staring at herself in the hall mirror, fingering the fake blonde tresses, such a weak imitation of what hers had once been. She slowly slid off her white fur jacket, pursing her red, red lips into a girlie magazine pout. As Marco moved up behind her to catch the jacket, their eyes met in the mirror. Elena laughed. 'You do look stunned.'

'Well. I didn't really expect . . .'

'Isn't it too much?' she pirouetted away from him down the hall and struck a pose, arms extended upwards, that showed off the tight, sequined sweater and slitted skirt. '*Ta Da.* Presenting — the new sensation. Come *on*, hum a few bars, help, any few bars, *ta da*, presenting the new Mina.' She stumbled through a few clumsy tap dance steps, pulled over an imaginary microphone and broke out into '*Sono una donna, non sono santa.*' ('I'm a woman, not a saint' — an old hit) in her deepest, most sultry voice. Then, just as suddenly, she stopped, holding the invisible microphone at arm's length, twisting her face to her right shoulder. 'Presenting the new me.'

'I wouldn't say it was you, new or otherwise. I didn't even *recognize* you at first.'

'And you, of course, would know.' She had resumed a more normal posture. 'But you're right. You see there's only one type of woman who's expected to be out at night. Expected so not noted. Not even a second glance from most. Venice used to be quite famous for its ladies.'

'So that's why.' Marco began guiding her towards the living room, letting his hand fall oh so gently on her shoulder.

'I cover all the possibilities. Oh, I know I shouldn't enjoy it. Those poor creatures. Though in a way we're all whores in this society. At least they . . . Still, the theatricality is sort of fun. You should have seen your face. What did you think?' She was looking not at him but at the tip of the cigarette she was lighting.

'I thought if we had the same thing in mind, you were expecting something more athletic, more dazzling than I usually go in for.' He let it slip out. The situation seemed so obvious. But Elena's swift change of expression showed that in fact they did not have the same thing in mind. Her face was uncertain, almost alarmed.

'Oh . . . of course, Marco . . . if that's what you want.'

Quickly enough, she regained control and presented a blank countenance.

'You didn't come . . .?'

She waved her hand towards the side table covered with neatly arranged bottles. 'Can I have some Scotch, please? Don't worry about ice.' Taking from the sideboard two of their best crystal glasses, he poured two generous portions. Her fingers brushed his as he handed her the glass. 'I came for your help. I thought I could trust you to help us.'

'If I can. I'll do what I can.' The Scotch was smooth, light on his tongue but was transformed into fire in his stomach. The old, beautiful Elena was watching him from behind the fringe of false eyelashes. Watching and judging. 'I'd never betray you in any way.' Layers and layers of blueness to her eyes. 'I know . . . I know who you are. I mean to say, we know you to be progressive, correct in your impulses. Of course we realize you are not *with us*. But better than those who blow hot and cold. Besides we cannot all be.'

'All be?'

Her laugh was an extension of her caramel voice, deep, delighted. Then, again she was serious. 'I won't be able to explain much. No questions.' She butted her cigarette with one sharp, quick motion.

'What do you want? I have to be allowed, at least, to ask that.' His stomach was starting to feel raw.

'I want to stay here tonight.'

'I presumed . . .'

'The truth is my friend needs a place to stay. No one would suspect . . . And I have to stay with him.'

'A friend?'

'A comrade.' She moved to the sideboard to help herself to another shot of Scotch.

Marco's hand was almost jerky as he moved

81

his glass up to his lips. The forbidden questions and the disappointment a muddle in his head.

'I need a yes or no.' She brought the Scotch over, refilling his glass.

'It's difficult, not knowing who I'm sheltering.'

'Such a small thing really. Wouldn't put you out in any way.'

'I don't know.'

'I remember when we were children you always stood aside from things. You would watch and make those drawings, the caricatures. They were good. But it seemed to be the only comment, the only attachment you could make. I mean, you would never join in — on the practical jokes — on the rhymes. I don't even remember you ever having a fist fight, while Tarquinio —'

'Why suddenly this?'

Elena moved closer to him, her bare arm lightly grazing his. 'It's your problem. You feel so superior — yes, you do — so "in the know." You stand back and judge. But that's the easy way. We have to do more. We are all responsible and we must all choose. You are either for the forces of progress, of life, or you are part of the rot.'

Her perfume was spicy, a bit oriental.

He took another sip of Scotch. 'You oversimplify. Besides, I do do more. Especially in my field. I work for the eradication of ugliness. For beauty.'

'Better buildings, better men?'

'I'm not part of the Van Der Rohe school. I believe in tradition, being part of a continuous line, making visible the best values of our culture.' He felt pompous even as he said it.

She moved still closer so her hand rested on his shoulder. Her perfume was persistent. 'Worse than I thought. What you do is design hotels that are pale imitations of already worn-out forms. Hotels for the bourgeois, where they play, isolated, protected from the people. Fantasy worlds. Nurseries for dangerous babies.'

He took a step away. 'Our choices aren't as narrow as you'd suggest. You and all your economics should know that.'

Her eyes were feverish. She reached out, her fingers gently caressing his cheek. 'Of course, Marco. I'm not blaming you. I just want you to see. A small gesture. What would it cost you? Who would ever know? A sign. A move in the right direction.'

'I was going to say yes.'

Immediately, she took a step back. 'I knew I could count on you.'

He caught her quickly — before she could slip again beyond his reach. This time he couldn't let her off easily. This time. He held onto her shoulders tightly, looking into her eyes until she gave way. A light nod. 'If you want . . .' He entered her aura of scent as he entered fog, knowing it had to be got through and that the familiar was there, somewhere. His lips on her face, her neck, her hands, searched for the girl he'd once held, for the clear-eyed child she, and he, had been. 'If you want . . .' It was what he wanted all right, this backward quest, what he wanted but not what he had imagined. He rubbed off the painted layer with his palm; the wig and clothes were shed, but her reactions remained skilled, almost professional. And he could touch only her skin, her hair, her private folds. Her eyes remained open, watching as if from far off.

He tried to hold himself back, but his body went on enjoying, crude fantasies fulfilled. The strong, firm flesh, the delicate, shapely features, the nipples springing up under his tongue, her head deft, accomplished in his lap, the perfume was now giving off undertones of incense and musk. 'Like an eighteenth century Venetian bazaar.' She smiled quizzically up at him. 'Your smell.' He covered her, wishing each inch of their flesh, forehead to toes, to touch, to embrace. He wrapped his hands under her buttocks, close and still closer.

'Wonderful.' She lied. 'Wonderful. It feels so good.' And the deceit was repeated, with each sigh, with each plunge repeated, until it took on a physical presence. It pressed, a dark weight, on the small of his back. It pressed hard and inflexible. Stone. While behind her assigned role, Elena became more fluid, more uncontainable. He could not hold her. Water. She was below and beyond him. She encompassed the city. His city, his beautiful city of illusions.

VII

'You really did help me arrive at the truth.' Marco could still hear her younger, higher-pitched voice. How old could Elena have been that night, fifteen? The two of them alone on a strange *terrazza*. A caressingly warm summer evening. She was wearing white, adding to her glow as she walked back and forth in the darkness, talking. 'You and Tarquinio.' No, he couldn't remember that, but she must have said it. They were waiting for the fireworks to begin; Marco, as always, with muscles tensed in preparation for that first bang. It was the feast of the *Redentore*, and though usually he spent it on the family boat (up and down the Grande Canale, over to the other side of the Giudecca, to San Giorgio, then to the Lido to watch the dawn over the sea — the natural spectacle completing the artificial one), this year he had escaped. How? One of those fights between his parents about his father's drinking or gambling perhaps. Common enough, but this one must have been conveniently close to the feast day, so his father had an excuse. And he had gone with Elena and her family to the house of their relatives on the Giudecca. Crossing the lagoon by foot over the bridge of boats, he and Elena were already separate, deep into a discussion of Gramsci's prison notebooks. They stood outside the great church as the rest of her family entered to light a candle in commemoration of the passing of the plague. And at the small, crowded flat, they quickly announced they would watch from the roof. Still, at the first explosion of coloured light, except for Marco's involuntary, almost strangled moan, they were silent; children again in the face of shooting pink stars and white unfurling carnations.

'Have some.' Elena pushed at him the plate of snails she had brought up with them. '*Bovoli*. They're really good.' Lifting the small white shells to her lips and sucking. 'Ummm. Do try.'

As he watched her perfectly formed mouth close and open, he felt a sensation — not quite pain, but a weakness and not in his stomach, deeper down. Elena turned back to a new display. A stylized lion hovering momentarily in the sky. He placed the hard edge of the shell against his lips. With his breath he sucked and it was there in his mouth. His stomach protested even before he could swallow, clenching in preparation. He kept his teeth tightly closed, gradually relaxing his jaw, letting his tongue touch the fleshy thing, then pushed it against the top of his mouth, feeling it slide down, a tiny paradox of soft hardness.

A new bang, a pink and blue storm of light possessing the sky, shattering into a million bright mosaics on the black lagoon. 'If you can stand the first few seconds, it's wonderful,' Marco offered, after finally swallowing. And Elena had laughed, both, it seemed, at the spectacle and him.

That easy laugh was gone, with the young voice, the young glowing face, gone. Yet, he was holding her naked body. He was free to trace the line of her shoulders, to caress a length of thigh. She was finally in the palm of his hand. He wanted to tell her, to give at least a hint of what it meant to him, but before he could begin to arrange the words, he could feel her flesh starting to retreat. She sat up and, with the covering of her body removed, he was suddenly conscious of the discordancy of his nakedness in the tasteful respectability of his living room. Elena was pulling out a new set of clothes and another package of cigarettes from her bag, exposing a wide, strong back and rather flat bum.

'Do you go in for this kind of thing very often?'

'Sex?'

'No. You know . . .'

She laughed. 'Liaisons? Sweet dalliance? How about you?'

'Actually, I . . . Not enough, not nearly enough.'

'But, of course, you envisioned that all of

us on the left spend all our time, all our energy fucking our brains out. Don't you know adultery is the pastime of the bourgeois? It provides a few thrills, a certain *frisson* to an otherwise meaningless life.' She was pulling up a pair of white cotton panties. 'A great social glue — adultery. Keeps marriages together.' Her face, still carrying the smudged remnants of her earlier paint, was serious as she rambled on, '. . . corruption, rottenness . . .'

As he slowly got up and began collecting his clothes, Marco found himself smiling his habitual ironic smile. 'I thought I'd be the one to feel guilty. After all, you're not married.'

'Guilty?' She sat down suddenly on the sofa, her pale body and white underwear startling against the black leather. 'Me? Don't be stupid. I don't feel guilty in the least. Why do you take everything so personally? I was speaking theoretically.'

'I wanted to speak of the past.' He walked over — a trifle self-conscious, a trifle cold, in his sky-blue shorts — to the side-table with the bottles. 'But I knew you would denounce me as nostalgic.' He handed her a refilled glass. 'It's just, our only link is the past. All right, our only justifiable link.'

'Justifiable? No. Marco, Marco, Marco, I don't allow you much, do I? . . . I don't deny our childhoods. There's no need to. Years of comradeship.' She drank the Scotch in two gulps. 'Come on. Sit beside me. We'll remember.' And, though edgy before the sudden contrition, he went and sat beside her. He was growing colder. There were goose bumps on his arms and legs, but to get dressed would have meant termination. 'I had to give you the correct line. But you mustn't think I believe in the false moralism the clerics peddle.' He wanted another try, another go-round. He needed to shatter her cocoon of words, to reach, undeflected, to her centre. 'Not at all. But one must understand the traps.' Her hand rested on his shoulder. 'After all, you are a man and I am a woman,' she wasn't smiling, 'and looking at it scientifically, there's no reason . . .'

He lifted her hand to his lips, using his tongue lightly on the long fingers. 'As you say, I'm a man and you . . .'

She pulled back smoothly, tucking her hands under her armpits. 'I do remember us, boy and girl. How we used to talk about what we would be when we grew up. You were going to be a world-famous artist and live in an enormous *palazzo* on the Grande Canale, "just like the Morosini."'

'Though decorated, of course, with more taste. And filled with even more masterpieces — mostly mine, but I would let a few old masters in.'

'And all the ladies of society would pursue you, praising your ability to show the hidden, the dark side of this city.'

'The blackness at the centre of the labyrinth. While you, with your voice, were going to be the most ravishing Mimi that La Fenice had ever seen . . . We didn't even get close.'

'Serves us right.'

'Why? For having dreams? For not knowing the world?'

'Oh Marco, for Christ's sake. We were hardly original. Our fantasies were invented for us by our circumstance. It serves us right for not knowing who we were and what we weren't.'

'We were children.' He started to rise but she clasped his arm.

'What were you thinking of? Before.'

'One evening of the *Redentore*.'

'Oh that. I'll never forget that, ever. It was the first year you moved into the palazzo. We must have been eight?'

'No. Later, much later.'

'You were sick in bed. I'll never forget it. I was with the adults and Tarquinio, up on the little *terrazza*. The fireworks had barely begun when we heard this scream; it was very very faint. At first we thought it was someone in a boat, on the canal. But then it came again. It was definitely beneath us, as if the stones of the place were crying out. We all rushed inside, of course. You were standing in the middle of the kitchen, in your underwear. You didn't seem to see us, as if you were still asleep, but your eyes were open. You were sobbing, but there were no tears. You just shook and shook.'

'You never told me before.' Thinking, no matter what mask he chose for himself, others saw him only in subordinate roles. The thick-headed servant. The cuckolded husband, the cowardly friend.

'You were terrified. I'd never even imagined such fear before. Your mother told us about the bombing and how the sound of the fireworks probably . . .' She was no longer playing. Her eyes were finally seeing only him and gently, so gently, seeing. But he had to get up and brush off her hand, cross the room. 'Even then I wanted to hold you. I never mentioned it or asked because it seemed so private, like I'd spied on you. But it really helped me understand something.'

The intermittent flashes of light. The merry-go-round still turning, the music off-rhythm, off-tune. The roller coaster. The neon lights of the fairground under the glare of explosions. A *luna park* more desolate than any landscape. 'They bombed Zara forty-three times. Forty-three times. What could be worth bombing forty-three times?'

'It was a centre of Yugoslav fascist activity. They had to. They never bombed Venice.'

'No. Everyone knew they wouldn't. She's untouchable. That's why we came back here. Safe harbour.'

Elena had followed him across the room.

Standing behind him, her long, cool fingers settled again lightly on his shoulder. 'Tell me about it.'

'What?' turning to her.

Her face had changed again. It was open almost avid. 'About the bombs. How it felt. What you saw. Tell me.'

When he couldn't even let himself remember, let alone tell.

'Tell me.'

He offered a diversion. 'We left on one of the last boats to Trieste. It was supposed to take only women and children, so my father dressed up as a woman. A black dress with white polka dots, front stuffed, a jaunty black straw hat tilted over one painted eye. When I saw him I guess I was so nervous, he did look good, I giggled. Just a few snorts. He slapped me hard across the face.' 'I can imagine. Your father.' It had worked. Her hand was on his cheek. When he pulled her towards him, this time, her body was unresistant, buoyant.

The doorbell rang, loud and eerie. Elena jumped away from him, grabbing at the rest of her clothes. 'It must be my friend. It must. I wasn't thinking. The time . . . I —'

Marco pulled on his shirt before pressing the front door button. 'Yes, your comrade.' Almost tripping in his haste to pull up his slacks, confused with visions of Paola purposefully treading up the stairs.

Somehow, when the knock at the door

came, they were both buttoned and zipped. Elena accompanied him down the corridor. 'When the bell rang, I thought we were discovered.' He used his ironic smile. 'What about me? Late at night, I always think . . . Even if I *know*. I expect a phalanx of uniformed men waiting.'

'We both suffer from over-dramatic imaginations.' Marco opened the door only an inch, the chain still on.

'It's him. It's OK.' Elena's voice was urgent. Still Marco hesitated, his hand pale and thick-knuckled against the dark shiny wood. Until, with a quick butting motion, her body hard with energy, Elena had displaced him, so that he stood slightly to the right, his arm still extended, his hand still trembling ever so slightly, and she was opening the door.

The intruder looked innocuous in his ordinariness. He was short, sturdy, dressed in a baggy green overcoat with a bulging right pocket, a cap pulled down almost to his eyes, a large canvas bag slung over his shoulder: a frequent type on Venetian streets. He hesitated, though Elena was motioning him in. He stood in the doorway, totally still except for his bottle-green eyes flickering back and forth between Elena and Marco.

Finally he moved. And the style of the movement, the knee-flexed steps, the hand on the bulging pocket, the alert head, clashed with the everyday familiarity of his Italian physiognomy. It was so obviously modelled on the American detective pattern, recognizable every evening on television.

Marco nearly laughed. He'd fallen not among thieves but among children, playing at danger, inflating their self-importance by paranoid fantasies. About to frame some witticism that would reassert his position, Marco's attention was caught by the trail of wet footprints down the marble hallway. He was going to have to watch the details. Paola never missed a thing. 'I have to insist,' he called out after the incongruous intruder, who had got as far as the living room, 'that you take your boots off.'

VIII

Half an hour later, Marco was standing in the doorway to the kitchen watching Elena and Piero (the name given) comfortably, so comfortably, seated at the kitchen table smoking cigarettes, drinking camomile tea. He had guided them there, away from the living room, when Piero announced he had to have a few minutes with Elena alone and, after Piero had closed the door almost in his face, had busied himself with returning the living room to its innocent state and preparing his study for night occupancy. The sheets were going to be the most difficult. He could just put them back in the cupboard tomorrow morning, though his fastidiousness rebelled at the thought. He had never learned how to use the washing machine, and besides, there would be the ironing. The neighbourhood dry cleaner could gossip. There was, of course, his mother. She would be pleased at being used in conspiracy against Paola. So pleased that it would be difficult for her not to make a small allusion to it whenever possible.

Elena's face was tired, her shoulders tight and hunched, but the hunch was companionable, angled in Piero's direction and, under the table, her right foot rested against his pant leg. 'What I'd like to know,' Marco kept his voice even, 'is about the sleeping arrangements. Do you need two beds or one?'

Elena's gaze switched quickly from Marco to her cup of tea. Piero had the annoying habit of pausing before answering a question. As if his answer were going to be of great import. 'Two beds.' His thick lips were pulled back in an expression of amusement. 'I'm sorry for all the trouble we're putting you to. We do appreciate it.'

The note of politeness, Marco saw immediately, was exactly the right one. It framed the extraordinary situation, giving him a handle so that he could carry it. He answered in kind, going on to offer food, towels, hot water.

'Toothbrush?'

'No extra ones, I'm afraid.'

'No matter.'

'You can use mine,' Elena offered. 'It's in my purse by the door to the living room.' There had to be something between them. What more inviolable than one's toothbrush?

'Most kind.' Piero was leaning back, feeling about in the pocket of his coat draped over the back of his chair. He pulled out a grey, hand-sized gun. 'If you'll excuse me.'

As soon as Piero left, Elena began praising him: his brilliant analysis, his ability to act, to clarify, to order. Marco only half-listened.

Elena's clouded, weary eyes, her lovely mouth, opening and closing — the words falling over each other the white cups on Paola's red patterned tablecloth, the dark corners of the cavernous kitchen — all were distant from him as if he were watching television. Only his stomach, caught on the sharp tooth of pain, did not feel the separation.

'Would you like some camomile? You are rather pale.' Elena had to repeat her question twice.

'No. I had some before you arrived.'

'That was a long time ago.'

'Very long.'

'I wish you could understand.'

'Understand what?'

'The party saved me; I searched and searched — you know. I had been, no, I had *tried* to be part of the struggle for a long time. But I was listening to the wrong people. I was deluded.'

'Now the delusions are gone? How can you be so sure?'

'Now I can see clearly; I have the *method* to enable me to see clearly. I was going mad. I was. Sinking into the rot. But now I'm on dry land.' Her eyes had lost the weary tinge, her face shone with the glare of her inner light. It was easy to understand just how clearly she did see. The world before those searchlight eyes would be either bright and clear-edged or blank and impenetrable. There could be no grey, no tricks of light and atmosphere, no Venetian reflections. 'I had a choice: go mad or join the party. Just like in the end, you have a choice, one choice. You are what I was. Sinking. If you could at least begin a dialogue with the right people.'

'So simple. The path of righteousness.' He didn't want to argue his sanity.

'Not simple. Clear.'

'Elena, I can never have your faith.'

'Don't be silly. It's not a question of faith.'

'Call it vision then.'

Elena screwed up her face, but before she could begin again Marco redirected their talk. 'Where did you meet Piero?'

She was immediately alert, suspicious. 'Oh, around. Why?'

'He seems an unusual man. Not at all the type that . . .'

He felt her relax.

'Oh, he's unusual. He was a professor when I first met him. Sociology.'

'An *assistente*?'

'No. He had a *cattedra*. He was one of the youngest ever.' She was so eager to praise him. 'He wasn't like anyone else. Even then. Piero didn't fool himself, and the students knew it. They all adored him. He gave up a lot.' Piero didn't look the professor type with his blunt strong features and stocky body, but of course that would add to the allure. Professor. It would give you a taste for power all right —

three hundred pairs of eyes waiting expectantly not for the truth but for the latest approach to chaos; each lecture hour, those pretty young women and pretty young men, not all three hundred but enough, hanging on to each word, each glance. Marco had hated all that part of university life, keeping aloof from the cliques, the admiration societies, the grey-haired icy professors unobtrusively in search of disciples.

Piero was back. Had he been listening at the door? He seemed to aim a frown at Elena as he drew the gun out of his pocket and laid it casually in front of him on the table.

'Would you put that away? I find it offensive.'

'It doesn't reflect at all on our trust in you.'

'I don't care a fig about that. It reflects a certain attitude, a certain philosophy that I have disagreed with, more, that I have been opposed to as long as I can remember. I value life above all. And you are in my house.'

Elena, surprisingly, shot him a sympathetic glance. Piero, his thick lips drawn back into an imitation of a smile, launched into a speech. It was a growing tendency: conversation not by dialogue but by speechmaking, not only among people like Piero and Elena but among all the educated of their generation. Piero was only more skilled than the rest. Obviously he had more practice addressing groups. His web of words was masterful, his voice always even, always gentle.

The argument itself was not new. The state was responsible for the greater, the more repressive violence. Not to protect oneself was to betray the people. Look at Allende. Even Gramsci had understood the necessity of forming a militia to defend party members against the Fascists. The necessary had to be done without weakness. Death must be freed from liberal mystification. As Lenin said, to kill or be killed is the easiest thing in the world. But he did not put the gun away.

'It's very late. We should try and get some sleep,' was Marco's reply. He held back his protest that it was exactly the easiness, the simplicity that he resisted. He was too lightheaded with weariness to attempt a no doubt useless rebuttal. The pain in his stomach was still strong, insistent. He could see Elena was also exhausted, the light switched off, her face fading into a uniform greyness.

But Piero was not ready to let them go. His praise for Gramsci's police was gradually shifting into a denigration of Gramsci. Why? Marco had never even joined the *Partito Comunista Italiano.* Or were the speeches so set that they had to be run all the way through?

Elena was suddenly up, clearing the table, rinsing out the cups. Of course. That night of the *Redentore* had only been the beginning of her profound passion for Gramsci. She had worshipped him for years. The prison note-books, in particular, were always prominently displayed wherever she lived, but she had studied each of his books so seriously. She even told Tarquinio once that she was considering changing her name to Tatiana in honour of Gramsci's faithful sister-in-law who had stuck by him when no one else did, who, in the end, alone had gone to the prison to recover his body, who alone had buried him. Piero was disparaging Gramsci for his dangerous liberalness. 'He was never a determinist and the results have been disastrous. He led to Togliatti and Togliatti to Berlinguer.' Piero's gaze was no longer impersonally concentrated on the air before him; he was staring at Elena. 'Don't you agree?' She did not answer, continuing to lay the rinsed cups on the drainboard that hung over the sink.

'Elena?' His voice was soft, almost sweet.

'Yes.' Drying her hands on a tea towel, she turned back to them. Her face was neutral.

'Yes?'

She seemed to take a deep breath. 'Gramsci did not understand historical determinism. He did not see that communism will be brought about inevitably but only by struggle and never by parliamentary bourgeois democracy. Or alliances.' Her blue eyes glanced for a second at Piero. Then she went on to offer more, in excess of what was needed, attacking Gramsci's emphasis on cultural hegemony.

Piero was rubbing his forehead slowly. The lesson he was giving Marco was not a political but a territorial one. 'She is mine. She bends her will to mine. She denounces all that she was for me. And I enjoy the possession, the bending, and I enjoy showing you how I bask in it.' If Marco had challenged Piero, confronted him on even ground, will against will, both Piero and Elena would deny that Piero had implied any such thing. Did their merciless light bleach out the subtle shades of human interchanges or, more likely, did it only prevent their acknowledging them?

Finally the flow of words from Elena's mouth stopped. There was an awkward silence, highlighting the outer sound of rain on water and stone. Only Piero, smiling his drawn-back smile, seemed at ease. 'Did you follow her? She did gloss over a few points. I am sure she is prepared for questions. She has a good analysis, a good grasp.'

'The correct line, I've no doubt. But at the moment I have to follow the best line for me, and it's drawing me to bed.'

Piero drew back his smile even wider. 'Of course, but . . .'

'It is very late,' from Elena.

'I still haven't made up a bed for you . . . in the living room.'

'I'll do it. Won't take me a second.' At the linen cupboard, Elena took the sheets and blankets from Marco with eagerness. 'Thanks,' she leaned over the pile and kissed Marco on both cheeks, 'for everything.'

Marco and Piero continued on down the hall, Piero still walking his alert, flex-kneed walk. At the door to the study, Marco could not resist an opposing sentence or two. 'You really think the people are willing to struggle, that your autonomous vanguard is truly expressing . . .'

But Piero interrupted him. 'The societal worker is with us. More than you could ever imagine. How could we act if it weren't for thousands of smaller, supporting actions?'

IX

The first time I tried to write of you I was fifteen. The summer before I had fallen in love with you. Do you remember? You happened to be broke, between jobs, between girls, so you spent much more time with me than you ever did before or again. '*Bambinona*,' you called me. Big baby. I almost didn't mind. Your voice was so gentle, so intimate when you said it. Besides, I was grateful. Riding the *motoscafo* to the Lido, then the bus to the cheapest beach — hour upon hour of talking. Lying in the sun, eating at cafés, sitting in your room watching you play your guitar. Hours upon hours. '*Bambinona*.' But you were the first man who attended to me, who let me tell.

In that first attempt at a novel, though, your role was preeminently symbolic. My main concern was in telling the story of 'a sensitive Italian girl' who emigrated, with her parents, to the prairies, who emigrated to loneliness and isolation, more, to an eventual mental and physical decay. For she was destroyed by the hostile, cold land. There was much dwelling, with no sense of contradiction, both on the emptiness, the ghostlessness and on the hostility, the cruelty of the prairie. I was to discover much later that all my personal, deeply felt comments, 'the cruelness of a straight line', 'the monstrous mountains', were the commonest of clichés. I had never read a Canadian book, yet I reproduced not only themes but images, lines.

You — Gianni was the name I gave you — represented Venice lost. Gianni was also an immigrant, a fellow 'sensitive soul', but one who retained, more, promoted gentle memories, old customs and habits. Still, Gianni refused to save my doomed heroine, leaving her and the wastes for Europe and a new, brilliant career as an opera singer.

Rereading that first attempt is embarrassing. I don't like being reminded of my adolescent, histrionic self. So tedious! But, sigh, we must own what we were as well as what we are. Besides, it illuminates the depth of the shock my family's emigration from Venice to Canada caused. For my life was split into two seemingly inimical halves, not only between the time before and after, but through all my growing years: Italy in summer, Canada in winter. Italy was enclosure, cocooning, the comfort of a secure place among the cousins, aunts, uncles, grandparents. There was always a surfeit of noise, of concern, of advice — of hands straightening the bow in my hair, grabbing me for a hug. A surfeit of regulations: 'You can't drink that, it's much too cold; you can't go out alone; you can't wear that dress; you can't, you can't. It's not *done*.' A surfeit of voices bouncing through the vague dark of those rooms shuttered against the summer sun and heat. Maybe because I was the youngest, you all turned me into the family pet; a doll to be dressed and decorated. My jewelry box is still stuffed with tiny gold chains, bracelets, rings. It was part of your childhood too — that closeness, carefulness, the insulating blanket of protectiveness, all springing from a hysterical perception of outside. Danger lurking at every corner, glowing from every strange eye.

Leaving Venice for the first time, I confronted ten days crossing the ocean, ten days staring at the limitless waves, three even more endless days on the train. Rock and tree, tree and rock. No houses, no people for hundreds upon hundreds of miles. The villages and towns where the train did stop seemed ill-proportioned, perched upon the land rather than rising from it. The only change came in the giving way to prairie — a land to my untrained eye still more monotone, still more desolate. Leaving Venice, though I was with Mamma and Papa, I felt stripped of family, of friends, of familiar walls and buildings, of proper landscape. I was exposed, alone in the nothingness.

Even the series of apartments and houses (for we moved constantly at first) seemed oddly open and bare, large windows on all sides and, since we couldn't afford appropriate furniture, large expanses of shiny oak floor.

Mamma and Papa, like many immigrants here, came not with the dream of a new land, of a new, freer world, but with the fantasy of quick profit, fast success. The financial losses caused by the war and the subsequent devaluation of the *lira* were to be recouped. Like most, Dad worked long hours. Mamma soon found staying home in the latest bare house in the latest bare suburb intolerable. 'I can't even go out for a walk in this cold. So I stare at that whiteness all day. You never see one living person walk by. Not even a poor dog.' Her hands would shake. Each time she served up soup or poured a glass of milk, some slipped down the sides. She began working as a waitress several evenings a week. She did not tell your mother or Aunt Elsa. Perhaps she was a bit ashamed. She was the educated one, and now she was reduced to this. Eventually, she did move up to secretarial work. Anyway, during those first few years, between Papa's overtime and English classes, and her waitressing, I seemed to pass most of my time alone, isolated.

The people here even stood farther away from each other. At the very first, the barrier of language kept me from my classmates. I remember my first school bus ride. We were staying on a farm near Calgary with distant relatives on Papa's side. I stood by the door, by the driver, unable to make my legs move forward, to make them move past those seatfuls of bouncing, fighting, dangling children. They were so different from the neatly dressed, controlled *bambini* of Venice, that I immediately judged them as wild and dangerous as the animals I had been told roamed the nearby foothills and mountains. Their collective smell, so totally new as to be beyond definition, pressed at me, wrenching my stomach. As an adult, I still try to analyze the components of that characteristic smell whenever I meet it on a bus or by a playground. It eludes me. There is dust certainly, junk food perhaps, whatever else; it still turns my stomach, still makes me faint in the head.

Then, on that first day, I was sure I would disgrace myself. Be sick there before them all. The driver was talking to me, pointing to a seat at the back. I carefully inched each heavy foot forward. It was hard to balance with the swaying, and I could not touch a seat in case I came in contact with one of those alien little hands. Their words seemed thrown, hurled at me, but when I tried to catch the sounds, they slipped, twisted away. A corner. I fell hard against a seat, dropping the lunch pail my cousins had insisted on. A big boy by the window in a grimy red jacket snapped his mouth open and closed. Then the others were laughing, watching, as I bent to my lunch-box, and laughing. Pulling back, I could feel it, away from me. Stranger. The laughter going on, newly fueled by the red-jacketed boy. The laughter not pulled back, pushing too close, too understandable.

I remember starting to understand the words. My first Canadian teacher, a wonderful, glamorous creature with red painted nails and three-inch heels, told the class, I thought, to bring shoelaces to bind the workbooks of pasted pictures we had made. I rode back to the farm unusually cheerful. I had understood — without repetition, without pantomime. My mother found me two brown shoelaces. But when the appropriate moment at school came and I pulled them out of my bag, I found all the other children had pulled out ribbons. Red, silver, gold-sparkled lace, velvet: a profusion of bright, beautiful ribbons and my dull brown shoelaces. I hadn't been totally wrong. I had understood the general idea. I could not deny my pleasure in that I was learning. But the triumph coexisted with the too familiar shame, the sense of being caught out yet again.

Gradually the mastery of the words, the proper understanding came. Mastery of pronunciation took longer. *Th* was particularly difficult. I took my turn at reading aloud and hearing, between my hesitant words, half-muffled giggles, looking up to see the exchange of knowing glances, the circle closing against me. 'Listen to her. *Dis*. Listen to her.' Round and round — laughs, whispers, secrets, gifts, birthdays — *shared*. I was left outside, watching.

I stood alone on the cold playground. The other girls skipped by the school. I edged towards them. Maybe I could slip in, blend imperceptably into the magic circle. But when I was standing silently beside them, their eyes shifted towards me. Their skipping song shifted smoothly from 'Spanish dancers do the kicks' to 'We don't want no DP's.' I was an adult before I discovered what the letters stood for. They had categorized me accurately enough.

It would have been easier if we hadn't moved so much those first few years. Besicker, Calgary, Leduc, Edmonton, Calgary. Twelve schools in seven years. Even when my voice, my words were just like the others, I never had the time to disarm the natural suspicion. It would have been easier if my parents had come here with the idea of staying. My mother in particular — well, you know how stubborn she can be, and she was determined that I would remain an Italian child. 'Do you want to be like one of these Canadians?' she would ask rhetorically, which meant, do you want to be without style, without manners, without sense? All Canadians called you by your first name as soon as they met you, ate horrible food that came out of cans, served dishwater instead of coffee, and drank rye whiskey with their meals, which was why, at the drop of a hat, they got disgustingly drunk. Besides, drunk or sober, they slapped you on the back and put their feet on the coffee table.

Any slip in etiquette, a forgotten 'thank you' or a fork carelessly picked up in the right hand, brought forth — with a punctuating sigh — 'you are becoming one of them.' I would beg her not to make me wear the clothes she had sent from Venice: a camel coat with black velvet collar, smocked woolen dresses, sensible leather shoes. I longed for ski jackets, jeans, shiny plastic shoes like everyone else's. But she was immovable. 'You aren't like everyone else. You should be proud of that. Even in Italy . . .' At school I did, of course, come in contact with other immigrant children, but my parents rated them on the same level as 'these Canadians'. It was no use pleading that Lucia's mother let her have a pair of blue jeans. Lucia's mother was from the South. You can imagine Mamma: 'You never know what crack they've climbed out of. You don't know, Bianca. Cannibals. South of Rome and you're in Africa.'

I withdrew to the fairy tale world I found in my favourite reading. I populated the gap between myself and everyone else with dwarves, giants, fairies, and elves. The empty spaces of our various homes became alternately the sea, a meadow, the centre of a mountain fort, a tower room. My involved stories filled the silence of the long hours I passed alone. My only memory of one town, a place called Stettler where we passed a few months, was of walking home through the snow. An old man coming in the opposite direction started and then smiled as I passed. Half a block later the same happened with a young woman. Only then did I realize I had not been running through my latest tale in my head but reciting it aloud, declaiming it to the snow-drifts, revelling in the sound of the words.

Eventually, we stopped moving. Mamma and Papa bought a house in yet another new area of Calgary. They began establishing a circle of acquaintances, even friends, most of them from the Veneto. Although there was no one else actually from Venice. 'True Venetians don't emigrate. They travel, but they don't settle,' Mamma pronounced, 'except for fools like us.'

And the daughter of one of these couples, Loretta, a round, dark girl with large expressive eyes, became my first friend. About once a month, on Sunday afternoons, the adults sat in our living room politely arguing Italy's past and future, inspired by sweet vermouth and ammonia cookies. Loretta and I would barricade ourselves in my room to keep out her three younger brothers and play out our latest fantasies with my Natalie Wood (her) and Sandra Dee (me) paper dolls.

One winter afternoon, outside their house, the earth and the sky all grey white; inside I was telling Loretta the story of a princess. This princess bore Loretta's name and general characteristics so that she would want me to tell, but the plot was for me. The princess had been kidnapped from her lovely palace by a wicked witch and imprisoned in a cold castle in a barren land. She was waiting for her prince — the King of Venice. I got no farther. Loretta was no longer sitting quietly in front of me; she was rushing around picking up bits of the Meccano set her brothers had scattered over the room.

'I'm not finished.'

'You're a drag, a gigantic drag.'

'A drag.'

'It's always Venice this and Venice that . . . Everybody knows it's just a rotten old stinking place.'

'Stinking? You don't understand.'

'I do so. Daddy says you Mazzins need to wake up a bit.' The brothers were standing by the door, attracted to the prospect of a fight. 'If Italy was as great for you as you guys say, why didn't you stay there? Huh? You can't smell your own crap, that's your trouble.'

I was standing now too, facing her. 'Well, my Mum says you're the type of people who have never had anything. You crawled out of the mountain rocks and now . . .'

'Can't smell . . .'

Then I was pulling her hair, wishing I could rip those thick curls right off her head. She didn't fight back, only shrieked, but all three brothers, even the baby, were aiming kicks and blows at my legs and middle, shouting: 'Stuck-up', 'Poop-head', 'Go back where you came

116

from.' I let go of Loretta. I tried to look dignified as I put on my coat and boots, but I wished I had pulled harder. When I looked back at their house from the sidewalk, Loretta and brothers were lined up at the window, each face distorted by the intensity with which they were sticking out their tongues.

Our friendship survived. I was flattered anyone could think I saw myself as superior. The parental friendship, however, did not. A few months later, Mamma was telling Loretta's father about the visit of several Italian journalists doing a series of articles on the 'West'. 'Such gentlemen, you don't find their type here. They all kissed my hand before they left.'

'And your ass, did they forget that?' was the reply. An effective termination.

I often shot off a rude comment myself in those years. I was beginning to feel that inevitable gulf between the immigrant parents and the child. I began to answer Mamma's 'Do you want to be like one of these Canadians?' with 'Yes, yes, yes.' I hadn't rejected Venice, but I wanted protective colouring. I wanted camouflage, to become like rather than to become. My parents' way meant exposure. Later, especially through Jody and her family, I began to see that Mamma's and Papa's judgement of Canadians was off and, more, that the code of rules, the method of behaviour they were trying to impress on me was inappropriate here.

Jody looked like she'd been formed in a

mold marked 'perfect Canadian girl'. She had blue eyes, a pert, turned-up nose, and a long, blonde ponytail that curled naturally at the bottom. She also had the widest crinolines, the biggest pencil box, and the most persistent giggle in the class. But it was in her home life that the essence of her glamour lay.

Her family seemed a model of calmness and rationality. I could never imagine her parents embarrassing her or her sisters in public. They spoke to Jody as if she were an adult. They even knocked before entering her room. The entire family, even the mother, spent an amazing amount of time in physical activity, skiing at Banff, skating, curling, tennis, swimming at the country club, riding at the stables. Jody had her own horse. Their house was big and, for Calgary, old, with an oak panelled dining room and tartan wallpaper in all the bathrooms, a view of the city, a trampoline in the backyard, and two Rolls Royces in the driveway. Their food, as mother had warned, often came from tins and packets. She hadn't warned how wonderful it would taste. Lipton's chicken noodle soup, ketchup, hot dogs, baked beans, barbecue-sauced spareribs, Jello, lemon meringue pie, Duncan Hines chocolate cake with Betty Crocker frosting, ice cream with Kraft marshmallow topping — a revelation indeed.

'We're Maritimers,' her father would say to me over supper, 'though all the children were born in Calgary. My father and his father before him worked the coal mines of Cape Breton. I worked there myself. Only a couple of years older than you. Every summer through high school and through law school at Dalhousie. Wouldn't think it, would you? It's a good country this. No limits. You can make yourself. Country of the future.' He would glance up and down the table to make sure each child had followed, registered again the family myth. 'Coal miner to corporation lawyer.' His eyes would seek out Jody's. 'Remember.'

Several times, Jody's mother invited my mother to her house for tea. The Canadian mother always sat straight-backed but slightly, politely, angled forward. The Italian one was looser, legs crossed, head turning, inspecting the room.

And each time, the Canadian one, her smile fixed, 'Won't you have more tea? Another biscuit?'

The Italian one, edging her cup a bit forward on the side couldn't. 'Oh, no, thank you, no. You have been most kind. But I couldn't. No.'

'Very well.' Long pause. 'That certainly is a nice blouse (dress, scarf). Did you get it in town.'

'Of course not.'

And each time, afterwards, Mamma would criticize long and loudly. Couldn't I see how impolite the woman was? She barely offered a thing. And didn't she ever express an opinion on anything? Dull, no doubt about it. I would try to explain that Jody's mother was being more than correct, that the elaborate web of flattering words, though standard in Italy, was alien, even suspect here.

'Don't tell me what's correct and what's not correct. I wasn't born yesterday. I've mixed with the best people. Have I ever told you what a close friend of the Countess di Toffoli I was before I was married?'

'Many, many times.'

'And not only her. But how are you to know? We should never have come to this barbarous place. Did you notice how *every* painting in that room was of a mountain view? Not that there are many other views of note here. A face would have been nice.'

Yet, typically, Mamma was not above using Jody's mother as an authority in one of her campaigns. She was against 'sock hops', afternoon dances in the gym for the grade eights. I was desperate to go, even though I knew no one would ask me to dance. (Just as a few years later I fought for the permission to date although I had never even been approached.)

'Those hop-hop things are disgraceful.'

'Hop-hop things?' Jody's mother's smile was frozen in mystification.

'Hops. Dances. They are only children — babies. We didn't have such things in my day.'

'*Mother*,' I was not supposed to talk, but

this was too much. 'You went to a girl's school.'

'And so shall you next year. Away from all this hopping. You wouldn't hear of such things in Italy.'

'*Mother*, things are changing there too. Anyway the schools don't have gyms.'

At this, Jody's mother angled herself a bit farther forward. 'Everything is changing so fast, isn't it? It makes one quite breathless. Look at how quickly Calgary is growing!'

This innocuous statement was all Mamma needed. For weeks I was told that Mrs. Stewart supported her, that she agreed about *those* dances.

Unlike most Italian immigrant women, Mamma had learned English relatively quickly; that is, she learned to use the words, to make the appropriate sounds, but she didn't learn the context, the web of social meaning. If the words sounded right, sounded as she sensed they should, her intended meaning must be there, no matter what I claimed. 'Crazy bones', she would call me affectionately, or she'd inform me, 'I've been working like a moose.'

For a long time, I didn't understand this. Since I saw that her judgement on things Canadian was off, since I heard her distortions, I believed that all she said, her whole system of customs and beliefs, was fake, a private fantasy, like the fairy tales I made up for myself. But then, during my summers in Venice, I would be surprised over and over to find that she could identify subtle shadings, that her methods of evaluation could apply. Even her stories about her younger self (the friendships with the aristocrats, the many suitors) would be confirmed, borne witness to by Aunt Elsa and your mother.

'Crazy bones. It's perfect. Your mother is so funny,' Jody would insist, 'not dull like mine.' Ironically, just as I wanted Jody's ordered, pastel life, she was envious of my summers in Venice. 'Tell me again about the canals and the beach. Come on. Tell me.' She was interested in the meals, the clothes, the TV programs, aunts, cousins, and, most of all, you. 'He does sound yummy.' With Jody, for the first time, I sensed how the two halves of my life could meet, the mask and the self fuse.

Yet, I still had no doubt that that self was Venetian. I wanted to belong here, but I was sure that I didn't, that I was, to use a phrase from that first novel, 'in exile in a bitter land'.

I remember that summer I began to love you; you always introduced me as *la mia piccola cugina canadese,* my little Canadian cousin, to your friends. And I would protest: 'Canadian. I'm as Venetian as the rest of you.'

But, of course, I wasn't quite. Once on the third floor of Da' Rezzonico, surrounded by painting after Longhi painting of daily life in eighteenth-century Venice, you had started by talking of the revolutionary use of colour by

Venetian painters, of underpainting and impasto, of glazes and golden tonality, and had gradually strayed into talking of your own paintings. 'Up until last year, I was convinced that I was a painter. I forgave myself a lot on that basis. I was an artist. I had to live life to the full. But last year I began to see my work wouldn't really do . . . Oddly enough, it began just as I began selling a few canvasses. I began to feel the massiveness of my limitations. I wanted to paint my city — the light, the fantasy. To say that it had been done better before is an understatement. What could I show that hadn't been shown before? I could only feel shame in front of the authentic . . . I have to make myself give up the role of artist. But what am I left with? I can't make a life out of being a hotel porter or a tourist guide. No, I must have a focus, a frame to pour the rest of myself into. I must. But what?'

All around me Longhi's women: red hair, pale pointed faces, dominating sharp dark eyes. My hair, my face, my eyes, even my round body reproduced over and over. Still, when I tried to answer you, the words on my tongue were English. I paused, I stuttered, searched for the Italian equivalents. I was smooth enough with the phrases of family and home. But theory, abstract thought, seemed necessarily English, for it was the language in which I read. I stopped in the middle of a sentence about the benefits of further education. 'I can't quite say what I mean. It's so frustrating.' 'On the contrary.' You had taken my elbow, bringing it to sudden consciousness and were guiding me towards the stairs. 'You do very well. Your accent is amazingly close. You can barely tell that you live over there.'

Barely. Later I stood in front of the mirror and practised. It was in the movement of my facial muscles and my mouth that I was caught out. But I couldn't loosen my jaw. My mouth wouldn't open wide enough to let the words properly roll. The Canadian style, tight and reserved, had been coded into my body and could not be unlearned.

X

Marco was dizzy with tiredness but as soon as he lay down in the four-postered matrimonial bed, he was awake, his hands and feet twitching slightly. Odd to be lying there without Paola. Even when their truce was shattered, when the anger was open and bitter between them and when he lay as close as possible to the edge of the bed to avoid an accidental brush with her foot or hand, still he expected her there. Her physical presence warded off the night terrors.

Once, Paola had gone to sleep in the study. The argument had begun over a comment of his mother's that there was nothing on their side that could account for Francesco's abnormality. Paola had all but ordered her out of the apartment. Though he felt irritated that she could not take with more perspective the comments of an old woman, he had understood her vulnerability. But the understanding soon faded under her barrage of words. For her attack quickly switched from his mother to him.

How dare his mother, an ignorant woman who still spoke in dialect? It was all his fault — he allowed his wife to be treated like the sole of a shoe. He didn't command respect for his wife. But then he didn't manage to command anything, did he? The old cliché hovered between them, 'if you were a real man —' She was standing by the stove heating up some milk to make some Ovaltine for him.

'No doubt, I wouldn't have to drink my *Ovomaltina*.' Paola's already bright cheeks flushed even brighter. 'Why don't you ever listen?' Marco shrugged his shoulders and began moving to the door. 'What about your milk? You know the doctor said —'

Marco rolled his eyes. 'Will you stop pushing it. Enough's enough.'

Paola let out a squeal, grabbed the carton of milk perched on the stove and threw it at him. It bounced off his chest and fell to the floor, spilling out over the tiles. 'There — you see what you made me do. Why can't you face something for once?' The intensity of anger and the loss of control were unusual for Paola. Marco couldn't let this moment of weakness pass. It offered the possibility of readjusting the balance between them.

He turned back from the door, picked up the carton and began reading aloud in Venetian dialect on the side.

'*Latte, latte, sempre latte*.' Milk, milk, always milk.

'Why do you have to turn everything into a joke?' Paola pulled the pan jerkily off the flame. 'And if I do push you a bit on the milk and eating, it's for your own good.'

'Tante Zebte, ancuo più che mai
Me par che i sia ben intossegai.'
(Many people, more than ever,
Seem to me well-poisoned.)

Paola had grabbed a cleaning rag and was on her knees, mopping up. 'You've never been a husband to me, not a proper one. More of a spoilt child.' Surely she didn't believe that. Surely, the words, like the bobbing back and forth of her wide bottom, were propelled by anger and by the scene.

'If you notice the atmosphere
Of either Venice or Marghera
Your wish to take a turn will pass.'

'Will you stop that?' She was kneeling beside his feet and suddenly delivered a sharp punch to his right knee.

He didn't let himself wince but kept on selecting appropriate lines.

'De bever late, magari ogni ora
Ch'el sia pur di vaca bionda o mora.'
(Drink milk, even any hour
As long as it comes from a cow
either blonde or brunette.)

He allowed his voice to pause on the *vaca*, pronouncing each syllable; he allowed his voice to glint. Paola threw down the rag. There were tears on her cheeks. Awkwardly, one hand on the table, she hauled herself up. With one last look, '*Bastard*,' she headed for the door. Still, he didn't let himself stop.

'Every moment is the right one for drinking milk,

As long as it is marked with the sign of the lion,' he called after her.

But he could not make himself follow, continue the skirmish, savour the temporary victory. He should have. He was always retreating too soon, always disarmed by the first sign of tears. He should have pushed on, pushed them both on until they fell into the centre, the common heart of their maze of sorrow. To face something for once.

That night it was as if his mind was freed by the absence of her body; the dreams were as thick and bright as fallen leaves. But it was a freedom he did not need. The dreams all had a brittle quality forecasting end, decay.

He imagined Paola asleep in Padova on a narrow, strange bed. Her face finally relaxed against the lumpy pillow, her mouth open. Francesco in a steel-barred cot. Surely they would have given him a shot to help him sleep. But Marco could only see him awake, his blank, puffy eyes wide open in the dim, silent hospital room. Did Francesco sense on some animal level that his fate was being debated, decided? Marco should be there with him. If the boy was awake in such a strange place, alone. Francesco had not reason with which to loosen the paws of terror. He should be there.

Holding Francesco's hand. Those damp stubby fingers.

'La Bocca sollevò dal fiero pasto.' (The mouth lifted from the proud meal.)

Again, the dark, convoluted *calle* of Venice. Searching for the centre of the labyrinth. He was not alone. Stepping silently from gondola to land, moving steadily along the edge of the stone palaces were cloaked and masked figures. Only their movement made them visible, for they nearly merged with the darkness. Occasionally, a glint of reflected light from the canal highlighted the long, curved nose of a Pantaleone or the cruel, strong features of a Pulcinella.

'La Bocca sollevò dal fiero pasto.' Elena's voice. But where? One of those masked presences hurrying in search of private, hidden pleasures?

Campo. Emptiness and bright lights. 'Save me.' The words were pronounced with a flattening English accent. Behind him, dressed in the clothes of Columbine, but unmasked, his Canadian cousin.

'Bambinona,' he called to her, but she stood still, watching him. 'From the mouth of the lion.' Watching. Someone else was joining her. A lace-edged mask, a cloak framing white shoulders and white, melon-sized breasts. Paola's breasts. 'The mouth . . .'

Elena's voice. Other figures gathering around Bianca and Paola. Their eyes glittering and watchful from behind the masks. He knew them and did not know them. He saw Adolfo's mouth, Tarquinio's stance, his mother's hands, but they seemed random details rather than identifiable characteristics.

'*Carnevale*,' Bianca's lips were barely moving. '*Carnevale*.' Carried away from them, upwards in a slow curve. The quiet filled suddenly with jangling fair music. Up. At the front of the crowd, beside Bianca — Francesco. Also maskless. 'Daddy.' His unclear voice floating up, through the din. Higher. Higher. And below him now the city, crouched, sinuous, sleeping. Apex. The lagoon, eternal, motionless meeting of sea and sky. Beginning. The curve down was faster, the music louder. He was on a gigantic unlit Ferris wheel. *Carnevale.* The inescapable. Down. Down. Raucous music. Farewell to the flesh. He knew. Farewell, for now he was flesh, falling faster, only flesh. Falling. The roar of the planes drowning . . .

Marco found himself standing, doorknob in hand, sweating, his tongue thick, his throat tight. He could hear the echoes of a scream still vibrating. Automatically turning back to see if he had wakened Paola, he found their bed rumpled and empty and he remembered. As he stepped into the hall on his way to the bathroom, a scream, faint, female, came from the direction of the study. She hadn't cried out for him. She had given him only a few practised moans and a polite smile. But he had only memory and his body with which to ignite her. Now she was hot with the vision of future conflagrations. 'Every utopia is possible.' That slogan, unsaid this evening but still heard. 'Every utopia.' Drawn up tight, tiptoeing down the hall, he saw Elena's mouth slack with pleasure, her thighs wet, her eyes dazed. Abandonment to the promise. Disgust flopped threateningly in his stomach; his mind writhed away from the cascade of pictures presenting themselves: close-ups of Piero's stubby fingers on Elena's breasts, his thick hairy thighs on her white legs, his buttocks clenching for the plunge.

Still, inevitably, Marco placed his right ear on the study door. At first he heard only the interchange of voices, the words obscured by his agitation, but gradually, as his heart began to beat more regularly, as his hands and stomach calmed, he understood phrases, sentences, entire replies.

Piero was forceful, excited. He wouldn't have told her if he thought she was going to be so stupid. There was a need for clarification.

Elena's voice was soft but animated. She thought it was too soon. Everything had gone so well today. Why again so soon, so close? How could they get a message to Beppi if Piero had to rush back to Padova and she was off to Genova?

'Exactly,' Piero again, 'we'll be far away. Safe from implication. Don't worry, I've made the analysis. Tomorrow is the appropriate day.'

Barely letting himself breathe, Marco crouched and peered through the keyhole. Again, at first, he could make out little: blurred colours, distorted space, but gradually, as he learned to shift his eye for different perspectives he began to see. They were sprawled on the small bed. Elena's fuzzy head rested on Piero's shoulder, but they were both dressed. Only their feet hanging over the side of the bed, were bare. Marco had wanted to see, to know, as a lesson to himself that he wouldn't forget. He had seen, but he still did not quite know.

Lifting his head edging away from the door he heard Piero's voice louder than before. 'But we can never be too careful. We must never trust. We are surrounded by spies. There is danger everywhere.'

Morning

XI

The tolling of the morning bells pulled Marco up from the well of unconsciousness. Still floating on that surface between sleeping and waking, he tried to count each ring, but he had no idea when they had begun; and before they ended, other bells, seemingly as close, began, filling his darkened room with a cacophony of sound. Every church in the neighbourhood from Frari to San Pantaleon must have been in the noisy competition, calling to the faithful. Only the call was too long. It was Saturday, not Sunday, and there was no peal of joy, just the steady insistent tolling, which hammered Marco's head to the pillow. Beware.

Then, the siren began, a blaring wail drowning out the earlier method of warning. Marco tensed against any possible Zara memories, but none came, only the memory of Francesco wailing in remarkable unison with earlier sirens. Until the outside blaring stopped, it was impossible to calm the child, no matter how much they cuddled or talked to him.

Acqua alta. High water. All over the city shopkeepers, families would be frenziedly hauling possessions to higher ground before the water extended its sway. And though he thought only idly of his *cantina* on the main floor with the skis, picnic basket, boxes of old clothes and books, the bells and sirens touched off a common sense of danger with his fellow citizens. Any relaxation and they would all be swept away. Unceasing work, unceasing struggle, were essential in shoring up the 'frail barrier' (as Venice was first called) against the claims of the sea.

Work, like pioneers staking out a new land.

Struggle, as his father and Tarquinio had, with the other men too young or too old for fighting, digging air raid shelters in Zara. Day after day they came home covered in red Istrian dust. Until the bombing began and that unity of purpose was shaken, exploded. Work: in the Palazzo Morosini during the *acqua alta*, the water insinuated its way in below the Istrian marble, crept up the brick wall past the layer of lead, up to the *piano nobile*, seeping out to the inner wood or plaster walls, peeling frescoes, staining the brocade coverings, accelerating natural decay.

The Morosinis did not generally use the *piano nobile*, living mostly on the mezzanine, and it was the floor that, when the Morosinis were away, became his private playground. Playing soccer with Tarquinio in the enormous, twelve-meter-high ballroom, sliding down the bannister of the great stone staircase, tricky because of the steepness but thrilling to zip past the fading Longhi frescoes.

Once he had tried the bannister not side-saddle, his usual way, but astride. He must have been leaning at a wrong angle, not using his hands as brakes. He was propelled off the end with such force that he landed flat and hard on his front. Stunned by the sudden impact, he hadn't tried to get up but had slowly rolled onto his back. He lay there waiting for his body to adjust, to start breathing normally, to stop crying, and his eyes were drawn inevitably to the fresco decorating the stairwell, seeing it, because of his unusual state, for the first time.

The fresco portrayed 'the fall of the giants', and later Marco would judge it to be a weak imitation of Michelangelo, a confused expanse of wrestling, half-naked heroes and giants, faded to invisibility at certain points and off in proportion and perspective in others for anyone standing at the bottom of the forty meter staircase. But then that medley of muscular arms and legs spoke to his early adolescent struggles for physical mastery. High up to his left there was a dark-bearded giant, his body twisted in air, his arm extended towards Marco as if he had just thrown something. As Marco lay, sprawled out on the marble floor, still hurting, it felt as if it were he that had been thrown. Not cast down in anger; the dark giant's expression, like that of all the giants, was benign.

No, cast down in jest. Look, you are also an object to be played with. That line between animate and inanimate, it can also waver, flow. Look. And he continued looking, his eyes straining to make out the details but looking ever upwards, following the sun. His muscles clenching as if ready for a leap. It was when, finally, he stared straight at the crowning glass dome, reflecting a dazzlingly blue sky, that it happened.

Something deep inside him seemed to tear, as if a gentle gigantic hand was pulling him in two, leaving a sentimental, floating sensation. He could still feel his aching body, like a gritty residue, but the torn part was expanding — both filled with that intense blueness and tossed up toward it.

But suddenly from the centre of that rising joy, an arrow of fear. He was being blown apart. He'd be found, bits of blood and flesh, plastered to the dome and the walls. Instantly, he shrank back to the floor. He lay, head spinning, the giants staring indifferently down at him.

The other incident came the next fall when he was thirteen.

Having persuaded Elena, before she went off with a group of giggling girlfriends, to get him the key, he was in the ballroom alone, not to play but to get away from the two-room apartment where every square centimeter was filled and tainted by his parents' angry words.

He was standing beside one of the tall windows, gazing down at the ragged, leaf-strewn inner courtyard, when he heard steps and voices from the direction of the great staircase. Thinking it was Elena's parents, he walked towards the sounds, ready with an explanation for his presence. But as soon as he got close enough to distinguish the voices, he realized it wasn't they. There were three men: one with a deep, mellow, educated voice, the other two with the rough, sing-songish voices of dialect speakers.

Marco pressed himself against the wall by the door through which the voices could be heard. They were obviously heading for the ballroom, though stopping to inspect minor points of damage on the way, since they were discussing the restoration of the gold flower patterns on the dark wood-beamed ceiling: Morosini explaining what he wanted done, the other two quoting prices. Remembering a few places where the peeling paint had been helped along by his soccer ball and remembering Morosini's manner the previous times they had met, an excessive politeness and interest belied by the cool expression ('And what is this young man doing these days? First form? Amazing.') he knew he must not be caught. If he tried to cross the ballroom to escape by the other staircase, he would be seen through the spacious doorways. The wall he was leaning against had had painted on it, in an eigteenthcentury renovation, a quartet of bewigged musicians, and Elena's father had told Tarquinio and him, the time he gave them a detailed tour, that it was in front of this spot that the musicians would play. Marco ran his hand along the wall. There — the bump of paint on the cellist's bulbous nose, a strong push and suddenly, where before there had been only wall, now there was a small open door and behind it a narrow stone staircase. He stepped in and pulled the door almost closed behind him.

The gambler's stairs. Elena's father had also explained that in the eighteenth century, on the upper floor where now the Morosinis' niece and husband lived, there had been one of Venice's most popular illegal gambling dens. Two secret staircases, for easy escape from police raids, had been added to the palace's charms. The other staircase had been damaged when the bedroom it terminated in had been sold, walls, ceilings, and all, to an American museum. ('The war,' Count Morosini had been reported as saying, 'was hard on us all.') But this one had been left literally untouched for the last two hundred years.

Marco sat leaning forward both to avoid the higher curving step that dug into his back and to peek through the crack and observe Morosini and the workers. They were in the ballroom, all staring up at the twelve-meter high ceiling, pointing, talking. The cold dampness from the steps and walls began to sink through Marco's scanty flesh to his bones. Those gamblers had at least had candles and obviously more layers of clothes. He could see them, streaming by one by one, light-footed, pale, with unnaturally vivacious eyes. His goose bumped skin could sense the silk of cloaks and swept-up skirts as they fluttered over him. The ruined nobility of Venice.

The aristocrat of the new, Austrian order, and his assistants were moving closer, examining the sorry state of the pale green brocade wall coverings. Reluctantly, Marco pulled the door to a complete close. The darkness was so total that it banished even the ghostly pleasure seekers. When he touched the wall to steady himself, he found it slimy. The smell was strong, soaking into him with the cold and the wet. As distraction, Marco tried to analyse the different essences: mold, spices, stagnant water. And the dusty odour of crumbling stone. So like the smell of San Michele. Bones. He was smelling the bones of the city.

Caught.

He doubled over, contracting his body so as not to touch the walls, so as not to cry out again. Caught. She had claimed her own. Swallowed him alive. He was caught in the mouth. Trapped in the rot. No way out. He could only go deeper inwards. Swallowed. No escape.

But the door popped open, letting in blessed light and the image of the Count. 'What is going on here? Do I have to find human rot in the walls too?'

There was quite a fuss. For a while it seemed as if Marco's whole family would have to move. Only after the parish priest came to plead on the Bolcato behalf was the punishment narrowed down to Elena and him. For the next month, he spent every afternoon under supervision rinsing the Murano glass chandeliers of twenty years of grime, or in the Morosini's dining room polishing the tarnish off ornate silver vases and bowls. Meanwhile, Elena was sent to special lessons in lace-making. She was to make a small cloth for the Countess's dressing table. 'It's most generous on the Count's part,' Elena's mother said, 'more of a privilege than a punishment.' Elena didn't reply, but she did, if she ran into Marco on her return from the lace school, swear at him. 'It's all your fault. You should have left me out of it.'

A knock at the door replaced the image of child Elena, red-eyed and shoulders hunched from that close, detailed work, with Elena on the edge of middle age, again with red eyes, again shoulders hunched.

'*Permesso?* May I come in?' She was carrying a tray.

'Might as well,' Marco pulled himself up to a sitting position, arranging the pillows behind him. Probably his breath stank and he needed a shave, but he could hardly leap out of bed and rush down the hall to the bathroom.

'Breakfast.' She placed the tray — two bowls of *caffè e latte*, two rolls of yesterday's bread, butter and marmalade — over his legs.

'Never been served breakfast in bed before.'

She had gone over to the two windows and was opening the shutters, allowing a soft grey light to insinuate its way into the room. 'I know that's not true.'

'Well, except by my mother. That doesn't count.'

'You men are all alike.' Sitting herself down on the edge of the bed, by his feet.

'I protest. I hardly ordered . . .'

'No.' Her irises shone out blue and sincere despite the redness of the rest of her eyes. 'I wanted to thank you for helping us. We do appreciate it.' She moved up the bed, closer to the tray. Her perfume, lighter than last night but still there, an aura of spices and flesh, floated over the space between them and caressed him.

'Has Piero eaten?'

'Oh, he's already gone. Luckily, he left just before the water began to rise. He suspected it might. We didn't want to wake you, so he asked me to thank you. Of course, after the sirens, I thought you couldn't possibly be sleeping.'

They both raised their bowls and took a

sip. 'He's an extraordinary man, Piero. It was interesting seeing you two together.'

'Yes, though you shouldn't think of "we two". It's not like that.' She had obviously been warned against revealing anything, but the impulse proved irresistible. 'He's totally dedicated. He's given his life. That's why these rumours are ridiculous.'

'Rumours? What rumours? I've never heard of him before.'

'Of course not. It was in the party — allegations that he was a plant . . . by the CIA or something. Some letters appeared. They were forgeries, of course. It was disgraceful. The dogs.' Marco restrained himself from telling her he wished that these running dogs had caught their prey or, a more cheering thought, that real hounds would hunt down her precious night companion.

'I know you think I am obsessed with the past, but I must admit, when you knocked, I was remembering when Morosini made you take those lessons.'

'Now that's something I remind myself of. It's so typical. Teach the poor girl a trade and what better than one that keeps her with head bowed for hours every day. And my mother wanted me to go on with it. I hated it so much. Do you know when I try to sew on a button now my hands shake so much I can hardly do it. The anger is that deep within me.'

Marco broke off a morsel of bread and cautiously offered it to his mouth. 'I'm sorry,' Elena was acting the hostess with a slight smile, 'that the bread is stale, but I couldn't get down to the bakery.' Since the first bit of food had been accepted by his stomach, he buttered the rest of the roll.

'What are you planning? It may be awkward if you wait for the water to go down.' He could imagine: Paola and Francesco met by a smiling, in-charge Elena.

'No. I have to leave. I can't be trapped here. I thought you could lend me some wading boots.'

Marco set down his coffee. 'How would you get them back? Paola would notice if they just disappeared.'

'You lent them to your mother? I could mail them to your office.'

'I don't know.'

'Look, I can't float out of here. And in my heels . . . It's either the boots or you're stuck with me.'

Marco shrugged his shoulders. 'All right.'

How intimate the scene would look to a viewer — the shared breakfast, both of them on the bed, she in jeans, he naked under the covers, their casual arguing. Only the light seemed off — so grey and hazy.

He shifted his legs carefully under the tray. The smoothness of the old-fashioned linen on his bare skin, the idea of the intimate scene, perhaps just the normal rhythm of desire in his body: something had sparked him. After last night he had expected a cure. Instead, treachery, his hands ached for wanting to reach out and grab her; once more, to touch and hold once more.

Elena was absentmindedly finishing the roll, her face young again in its relaxed musings. A blob of orange marmalade stuck to the corner of her mouth. Marco leaned forward and wiped it off with his napkin. Her smile was dazzling, sunlight in that grey room.

She had come to him in falseness, the truth of her elsewhere. But what about him? Hadn't he been trying to prove something? How many men and women came to each other as they should, desire springing from their centre? Instead of from surface titillation by programmed caresses, mental fantasies, or the vaporous sentiments of young lovers. They were probably the worst. Their delusion was the deepest. 'Romantic love', as if it wasn't the reflection of themselves in their lover's eyes that they loved, as if it wasn't the postures, the trappings, the masks, they wanted. 'We are unique.' As if inside we weren't all alike; individuality only through abnormality.

And he wasn't exempt. How often had Paola reached for him in the night and he had to stifle his first impulse to brush off her hands. He had to prod and titillate his indifference with fantasies and will. So he answered her with worked up, with cosseted feelings, rarely with true response. Dutiful husband. Loving wife. All appearance and no insides. There was pleasure, hot and even strong, pleasure of the nerve endings. Not what it should be, true and impersonal, man and woman.

Disgust, a cold lump in his stomach. Disgust at the whole abhorrent frantic business. Elena was waiting for him to put down his coffee bowl. She was already finished and anxious; her eyes inquisitive, her fist clenching and unclenching on the blanket. 'I put the sheets back. They were quite clean so you don't have to worry. The kitchen's back to normal. And I dumped all the cigarette butts out the window.'

'Thank you. You are such a careful, considerate pair.'

'I've grown good at erasing clues. It seemed easiest for me to do it. But you should check, you're more familiar with how things should be.'

'You want the boots?'

'Look, handsome, I have no desire to be in Paola's shoes, elevated as they might be. But necessity is necessity, and it is getting to be that time.'

'Schedules call?'

She didn't answer but handed him his dressing gown from the chair.

He found the spare boots at the back of the hall wardrobe. She pulled on her jacket, the silly fur one. 'I wish . . .'

She put her hand on his lips. 'No bourgeois romanticism.'

'I had no intention . . .' He was indignant.

She was pulling on the long, rubber boots. When she straightened, she left a light kiss on his cheek. 'Comrades in the revolution. We are now, you know.'

Marco stood at his front door and watched her clumsily descend the stairs. She was an odd figure with the jacket, the too-large boots, the fuzzy hair, her bulky purse over one shoulder, the heavy canvas bag that Piero had brought under the other arm. It was only when she stopped at the first landing to toss him a last comment, 'All this and a flood too,' that he suspected that the canvas bag must be stuffed with bank money.

XII

Marco closed and bolted the front door. He carefully checked room after room to be sure that everything was in its proper place. He started *The Four Seasons* on the record player. Then, and only then, as he sank into the sofa and those first notes rang out triumphant, was he overcome with relief. They were gone. He was alone with no duties until Paola and Francesco arrived at Piazzale Roma. He put his slippered feet on the coffee table. He didn't even have to get dressed. He would listen to records, as loud as he wanted, sketch a bit. If he could concentrate. If he could draw anything besides the line of Elena's shoulder, the curve of her bare arm (when she ruffled her hair), the compact roundness of her breasts. She was a broad, heavy rock damming up the free flow of his mind. It was so tidy her turning up when she had, the one night when Paola was away. But how could their meeting in that café not have been accidental? How could she have known? Had one of her little band designed some wondrous machine, a type of divining rod, that sought out vulnerability? Beep, it had gone when he had happened to cross its path — beep, beep — identification: moving target. No, perhaps sitting duck was the appropriate tag: sitting, waiting, unaware, unable.

The phone rang.

'I hope you're not planning to go out in this. And Francesco? Will Paola have enough sense? It's terrible, terrible; the water's coming through the bottom of the door. Every year it's worse.' His mother spoke so quickly that the words seemed to knock into and fall over each other like tin soldiers.

'Do you need help?'

'Aren't you listening? You stay home. I've moved everything. I tried to call Tarquinio, but his phone was busy. Who could he be talking to for so long? It must be Lea. You know her, loves to gossip. Or Patrizia, though it does seem a bit early in the morning for her.'

'I must ask you a favour.'

'The siren was only four bells, so it should stop soon. Start going down. I hope. I don't understand it — it's January, not November.'

'Mamma.'

'What do you want?'

'I had to lend out some wading boots and I'm going to tell Paola that I lent them to you. Do you understand?'

'I'm not stupid. You want me to lie.'

'I doubt she'll even mention it, but just in case. You dropped in this morning. The boots you had weren't adequate. You can think of something, I'm sure.'

'Who did you lend them to? That divorcee who lives in the apartment above yours? You always did have a weakness for blondes.'

'Yes, I did actually. But don't get me wrong. She was stuck. And you know how Paola is. I thought it would be easier . . .'

'I always knew that blonde was out for what she could get. You let people get familiar too easily. You should be careful.'

'Mamma.'

'Don't worry. I wouldn't give Paola any other reason to sink her fangs into you.'

'I have to go.'

'Someone's there?'

'The coffee's probably boiling over.'

'I should come over, make you a nice lunch. A little broth, a soft coddled egg.'

'And the water? Besides, I have work to do.'

'You have to eat.'

'Tarquinio said I can drop in there if I want.'

'They didn't say anything to me. It's your Aunt Elsa; she's always been against me. Even last night, after you left. I was trying to reason with Patrizia about the makeup and the boy she's been seeing — her mother's heartbroken, you know — the way she carries on; it's inevitable, she'll come to a bad end, just you wait and see. Anyway, Elsa started in on me. Telling me that it was none of my business and that I was making it worse. As if she knew; she doesn't know what it means to be a mother. So now, I said, *now* I'm not even allowed to speak —'

'I can smell the coffee burning. Must go. Call me if you need any help.'

Marco put the needle arm back to the beginning of the record, turned the volume up and settled back on the sofa. He wished he still smoked, not from any bodily urge for a cigarette but because it seemed an appropriate accompaniment to his state of mind. Perhaps he should go and put on some more coffee. But before he could rouse himself, the music began to play on him.

Once, on a Sunday walk, when Paola had been pregnant with Francesco, they had found the Piazza emptied, all the people confined by police to the sides, in preparation for a historical parade, part of the celebration of the Regatta of the Four Maritime Republics. The square, unobscured by the usual crowds, was exposed in all its beauty. 'The living room of Europe.' Two thousand years of history: Greek, Byzantine, Gothic, Baroque, coexisting in harmonious balance, a melody of man's potential.

Then, as if giving voice to the emotions of the viewers, over the loudspeakers attached to the church came the first notes of 'Autumn' from *The Four Seasons*. The pigeons scattered over the square, in unison flew to a central spot and, as a flock, flew back and forth across the Piazza and Piazzetta controlled by the rhythm of the music. Paola took his hand and pressed it to her belly where he could feel their child kicking out as if it too could hear and respond to the glorious notes. The pigeons flew gradually higher, a grey blur before the glittering church, the gold-encrusted clock, higher into the deep blue May sky, interweaving by their flight the songs of the square, the music, the child-to-be into an almost heavenly cantata of human possibility.

The phone rang again.

'It took you a long time to answer.' Paola's voice wasn't quite as neutral this time. He could hear the slight hysterical edge.

'I was in the *salotto* listening to music.'

'How nice.'

'You didn't sleep?'

'Some. I took a pill. But I still tossed and turned.'

'I should have been there . . . And Francesco?'

'He seems all right. The other specialist is with him now.'

'They haven't told you anything?'

'Not much. But I think it's worse than we thought.'

The cold-eyed men. Merciless. 'No, not worse. I knew . . .'

Her voice cracked ever so slightly. 'You always know — don't you?'

'Paola.' Silence. 'When are you coming home? We can discuss it properly then.'

'I was going to take the 2:05 train, but I heard the water's high. We can't expose Francesco to . . .'

'It's not too serious. You can call just before you leave, see how it is. I could always bring boots to the station. We could get a taxi.'

'Don't you understand? We can't take risks.'

'And I'm saying there'll be no risk. Look, if you don't come home, I'll come to Padova.'

'I'll call you.' And, in a very Paola-like move, she hung up.

'Worse than we thought.' He *had* known, known that the white-masked men could only find the worst. Their rubber-gloved hands probed for the flaws in the machine. And in a child who was essentially flawed?

Poor Francesco. A hole in the heart. Ironic since if anything he was 'all heart'. Jammed full of indiscriminate affection. '*Bacini, bacini,*' kisses, kisses, was his most frequent phrase.

It had taken Marco and Paola six months before they had conquered their bitterness enough to have Francesco baptized. Before the service began, with the whole family standing around the baptismal font, Padre Lino had taken a sleeping Francesco from Paola. He had held him, smoothing down the voluminous skirts of the lace-embroidered baptismal gown. 'I have thought much about this child and children like him. But only recently have I seen that the birth of Franceso is a cause for rejoicing. For God has sent you a saint. This child will never know sin. What more could a Christian parent want?'

'Everything,' Marco had wanted to shout. But, of course, he hadn't. The service had gone on. Marco and Paola had renounced the devil and declared their belief in 'the forgiveness of sins and the resurrection of the body' on Francesco's behalf. Certain things were not done. Oh, Marco would have liked to have accepted this salve for the wound, but he had been without belief for so long. Still, now, after watching Francesco grow, after hearing his laughter, seeing his eagerness to please, to love, he understood what Padre Lino had meant. Blessed are the innocent. And the doctors, they did not judge the value of simplicity of heart. No. Their judgements were based on genetic codes. 'If only we'd tested when Mrs. Bolcato was pregnant,' one of them had said, 'we could have arranged for her to go to London for an abortion. No problem at all.'

The phone rang like an alarm. His body contracted in surprise. His hand was still resting on the receiver. '*Pronto.*' Marco could hear a blended roar, trucks, cars, and people, but no answering voice. '*Pronto.*'

'Finally, just as he was about to hang up. 'Marco?'

'Yes. Who is this?'

'Your overnight guest.' It was Piero, but his voice seemed distorted both by background noise and by nervousness.

'Yes.'

'A message must be carried to a friend. It's very important.'

'I'm sorry but I'm very busy. My son is coming home and . . .'

'I realize that but this must be done.'

'Not by me.'

'Look,' Piero's voice went slightly higher in register. 'Your wife has had enough to deal with these last few days. It would be unfortunate to agitate her further with more disappointments.'

'What are you getting at?'

'Listen. I have a letter here with certain information . . .'

'She won't believe you.'

'Certain details, a mention of a certain arrangement of objects in your bedroom to show that the writer . . . and there are the boots.'

'This is despicable.'

'No,' he raised his voice a bit to be heard over the growing background din. 'Just a necessity.'

'How long will this go on?'

'This is the only time. Once the message is carried, I'll destroy the letter. You have my word.'

'Not very reassuring. Why should I believe you?'

'There is no other way.' But Piero's voice had an uncertain note to it. 'Now listen carefully, we're running out of time. Go to the Bellini room at the *Academia*, at 11:30 this morning. There'll be a young man in a black coat and a red plaid shirt. Begin talking to him about one of the pictures. Then, casually, you must say to him, "This is a time of action." If he answers "a time of terrible beauty", tell him, "if the water is down, the demonstration begins at 16:00."'

'That's all?'

'Yes. Everything clear?' Marco repeated the instructions and the message.

'But nothing's clear. I didn't agree to . . .'

'The agreement was made last night.' And Piero, like Paola before him, had hung up, leaving Marco with his mouth open, words shrivelling in the back of his throat.

XIII

The second time I tried to recreate you, I chose more vivid and lurid colours. You were still the charming and suave representative European, but I added a touch of degeneracy, a central seed of corruption. My heroine, this time, was Canadian. She was a Joan Baez look-alike travelling in Europe. Her main characteristic, of course, was her innocence. Naturally, she was seduced and abandoned by the European, set on the path to her destruction. (A well-worn plot, this one.) I was titillated by the idea of 'destruction', which I associated with Dylan's 'Like a Rolling Stone'. I thrilled at imagining myself desperate: on the streets and at the mercy of any 'mystery tramp'.

Are you amused at being painted as a carrier of corruption? Let me plead age and circumstances. My parents were overprotective. In the face of unfamiliar and therefore suspect customs, they kept me reined in, bound and blinkered. They would not acknowledge that habits and guidelines could have changed in Italy since their youth. They clung to 'their way', but disconnected from the society it expressed, 'their way' shrivelled to no more than a dry bone of belief, no more than a skeleton of a once vital form. Even my school was more extreme than the school I would have gone to in Venice, reinforced as it was by the pervasive Canadian puritanism.

The semi-cloistered nuns told us over and over that it took only one step for all to be lost. Exposing our arms in sleeveless dresses, exposing our toes in sandals, or our knees in short skirts, any kiss that lasted longer than ten seconds — all sins of the flesh. Mortal sins. We were exhorted to envision our souls as black voids with not one speck of light left. Mortal. We must know that men were animals, that birth control pills caused deformed children, that venereal disease was rampant, that our private parts would drop off. Mortal indeed.

Is it any wonder, with daily doses of such propaganda, that I envisioned you a practitioner of perverse and multi-partnered sex? My novel was suggestive but vague since my concept of such practices was distilled from *La Dolce Vita* and from a couple of magazines I found in the back of a closet at a house where I babysat. The film in particular led me to believe that sexual evil occurred at parties where men rode horsey on the backs of large-bosomed women.

Books in the school library were heavily censored. Black paper was stuck over offending pictures in classical art books. Lines, pages were neatly inked out not only of novels but works of history, verse, and psychology. Yet when we held the pages up to the windows so the light shone through and managed to decipher a few words through the blackness, we found the forbidden to be innocent, even to our naive eyes. 'He took her into his arms and she melted against him.' Anything meatier would not have made it into the library in the first place. One girl was caught reading a James Bond book. Mother Elizabeth suspended her for a week and called her an agent of the devil in front of the whole class. I felt only thankfulness that it wasn't me, though neither Loretta, Jody, nor I would have had the nerve to buy a book 'like that'.

We complained about the nuns, but our indoctrination ran deep. Mass every day of Lent. The rosary every day of the year. The wooden beads on my fingers, the soothing words of the Hail Mary, repeated and repeated. Every ounce of what I was concentrated in worship. Safe and alive in worship. Bead after bead, prayer after prayer. Contemplate the wounds of our Lord. Contemplate his suffering. 'Imagine the nails in your hands, your feet,' Mother Geneviève would say, and I would imagine the thorns, the whips, the nails. I would see the lance piercing the side. We had no trouble imagining or being exalted by our imaginings. We thirsted for tales of the saints, tales of hair shirts, self-scourgings, castigations of the flesh — so repulsive and so satisfying.

My favourite saint was St. Maria Goretti. Jody, Loretta, and I read her life story repeatedly to ourselves, to each other. A martyr at thirteen, the glory of it. A martyr to foul male lust. She was good, she was beautiful, as we were not. Her very presence had inflamed a man to violence. We dwelt on each word of the death scene. 'No,' she had screamed, 'never.' So he had taken her with a knife. Twenty-four stab wounds. The frenzy of those plunges into flesh. And as the knife entered, as the blood poured out, she had not forgotten to hold down her skirts, to protect her modesty. 'A woman's modesty,' my mother would insist, 'is her most prized possession.'

'I'm sure I wouldn't have cared who saw my legs, not if I was dying,' Loretta said with a sigh.

'I would have just let him go ahead and have his way,' Jody added. 'I know it. I'm a coward.'

Maria was not only of better, stronger stuff than we, she had been blessed with faith that transforms, sanctified by action and belief beyond us. Which was why we read of her and no one would read of us; which was why she was canonized and prayed to by not only thirteen-year-olds all over the world but by her murderer. I had seen his picture in one of Mamma's magazines. An old man now, in a monastery cell that featured a shrine to his victim: 'I pray to her every day,' he said.

Deny the flesh and one was rewarded with devotion — devotion even of the flesh. 'Don't ever let a man touch you,' was my mother's contribution to my sex education. 'Men are all alike.' A touch, a kiss, even letting go of one's skirt and one was over the edge. Danger. The easy fall.

Do you see why in my sixteen-year-old fictionalizing I judged you degenerate? I remember those sun-filled beach mornings. I can still hear your cool voice with its amused edge, tracing out what I now know to be the old arguments. Sex was a basic appetite like hunger and thirst, and the satisfying as necessary. It was repression that twisted and dirtied. The church has mounted an enormous scaffold of lies to control and to oppress. It was a question of naked authority, naked power. You told me of the secret passage between a church and a convent in Mestre — a passage lined with skeletal products of priestly visitations. You piled up cases of infamy. You even hinted at long-buried indiscretions of Aunt Elsa and Lea.

We were sitting at a table in the beach café, shaded from the noonday sun by the giant umbrella. You were squinting at the sea. I sipped at my *granita di limone*, letting each sliver of sour ice loll on my tongue until it melted. 'These things happen. Why do you think we were given bodies? Don't be fooled by the dissembling.' How casually you aimed blow after blow at my crystal castle of beliefs. I grasped the long cold glass tightly. I was afraid you would laugh. *'Bambinona.'* But you didn't come close to noticing. My castle was shattering into sharp glass shards. You stared at the sea.

I wanted to demonstrate to you my coolness, my sophistication. But what could I say? I was having trouble keeping my voice steady. As usual, I fell back on books. 'I did read this book, a historical novel set in Restoration England. There was this girl . . .'

You were twenty-four and closer to the *Vitelloni* than to *La Dolce Vita*. I felt you had debauched my mind, but had wanted you to debauch my body.

I was so restless, edgy, the night Auselia, husband, and kids were visiting and I was put on a cot in your room. It was hot, the air heavy and stagnant with humidity. You were out late with friends. I lay on top of the white, slightly rough linen sheets and waited. My nerves twitched, jerked me back each time I began drifting towards sleep. Repeatedly I sat up and peered at your clock radio. I was caught, suspended in each moment. Yet, when I checked, I would be surprised — half an hour since I last looked, fifteen minutes, then ten.

Finally, you slipped in, so quietly that I thought for a moment that I had conjured you from an excess of desire. You sat, a dark form, unmoving, hunched on the edge of the bed.

'I'm awake. You can put on the light.'

You flipped on a muted sidelight. 'What's wrong? Can't sleep?' 'No, I've been lying here for hours. It's past two.' Your fingers were slow on your shirt buttons. Your face unusually sallow. 'But more to the point, what's wrong with you? Too much wine? Too much good time with the boys? No, it must be a woman.'

You stood as you pulled off your shirt. I was used to seeing and used to wondering over the extraordinariness of your body. For your frame is the frame of a large solid man, and your flesh is too scarce to properly cover it. Undressed, you seem, in your thinness, in the prominent pattern of bones on your skin, in the thick-ribbed scar on your left breastbone, vulnerable, exposing as you do what for others is hidden. And in the half light, far from the self-consciousness of day, I longed to touch, to know the vulnerability.

You sat again, on the other side of your bed, your back to me, edging down your pants. 'My stomach. Very bad.'

Steps in the hall. Your mother intruded into our room, going immediately over to you, fussing, insisting she would bring you camomile tea, milk, painkillers, anything. The argument must have started before, in the kitchen perhaps. You were firm, distant. Her pleading was gradually evolving into a tirade when she happened to look down at me still sprawled on the sheets in my gauzy nightgown. 'What are you doing, Bianca? Cover yourself!' She nearly flipped me off the bed by the brusqueness of her tugs at the sheets. 'What are you thinking of?'

'Mamma.' Your voice was suddenly sharp. 'She's a child.' Indignant, I pulled the sheets up over my fast-reddening cheeks. You were both wrong. I had no malice, no forethought. Yet I was not a child. And I knew you knew that. You had lied. In spite of all your talk of health, of openness and freedom, you refused to acknowledge the true contours of my shape and my mind. That refusal, I see now, foreshadowed a future stance, a future understanding. It was a stance that submitted neither to the authority of the old rules of priest and confessional nor to the authority of the new system of psychiatrists and 'bringing the truth to light'. It was an understanding that sex was indeed as dangerous as the nuns had taught me. But that danger was not the peril of sin, ''Tis better to marry than to burn.' No, it was a subtle, twisting danger. Your refusal sprang from a foreknowledge that sex could be treachery and illusion or the joyous core that impelled, that was life. And always requiring not so much honesty, openness, as care. Care.

So, in the dark, we lay on separate beds, our words a floating bridge across the room. You had taken several pills. Either they or the pain caused you to speak hesitantly with long pauses between each word. You spoke of your ulcer, the pains that began in early adolescence, the stomach operation at fourteen. I was still distracted by my embarrassment and by my consciousness of your body stretched out there just across the room. Yet even in the pseudo-intimacy I was so open to you that I felt each word. I knew your pain. The identification was so strong that when I returned to Calgary and began having stomach pains, I was sure that they were not real, only sympathetic twinges. And when the doctor insisted, X-rays in hand, on his diagnosis, I believed that your words had become flesh. They had penetrated to my centre and imprinted the pattern of your experience on me.

Don't be embarrassed. I know you did not realize the extent of your influence. It was not reasonable or predictable. Again, I plead age and circumstances. I was little more than a blank page. Still, you could have been a bit more aware. You could have recognized; you had been in my place just a few years before. You knew what it was to be taken over. (Elusive, elusive Elena.)

Oh, I know your intentions were honourable. You were simply playing the mentor to your little cousin, replaying the role Tarquinio had sketched out with Elena. You lectured me on painting, music, and politics. You condensed and simplified Marx, Lenin, and even

Proudhon. Most of all, you encouraged me to think, to question. 'They lie. They lie all the time, so you must ask, doubt, judge for yourself.' How often did you say that to me?

At lunch the next day, perhaps in compensation for the night's embarrassment, you offered to take me to see a performance of *The Merchant of Venice* at La Fenice that evening. I had never been out with you in the evening. I had never even seen a play. I pushed away the plate of *scampi risotto* I had been so dutifully consuming a moment before. I began tying knots in my linen napkin. 'Shakespeare? That would be too wonderful. We're going to be studying that play next year in school.'

'Calm down, Bianca. Eat.' Your mother was still cautious about the two of us.

'No way. I couldn't. Not another bite. Shakespeare . . . in Italian. Oh well. I guess I can't have everything. What should I wear? I have nothing . . .'

You had been smiling at me since you made the offer, but now your smile deepened, became less amused and more gentle. 'Your prettiest dress, of course.'

I spent an unprecedented half an hour getting ready that evening. Whitish lipstick and black eyeliner (borrowed from Lea), back-combing and a pink bow in my tightly permed hair, and my pink chiffon grade nine graduation dress. I thought I looked at least five years older and terribly sophisticated. You didn't compliment me though. You looked me up and down with a quick nod. 'Umm. Come on. We have to go. We're late.'

It was during the first intermission that I became self-conscious about how I looked. I was standing alone in one of the reception rooms, you having gone off to get two cokes. In front of me was an elegant, silent older woman and three chattering girls of about my age. Those girls were so perfectly finished. They were creations. Their puffed-out hair, their skilfully painted faces, close-fitting dresses, bangled arms: beautiful creations that appeared natural, artless. I felt so rough, so raw.

'Why the depressed look, little one?' You had returned, cokes in hand.

I gestured towards the girls. 'They make me feel so wrong.'

'Nonsense . . . You aren't what you could be . . .'

'I've never had any illusions about my looks. I know I'll never be much.' True to adolescent form, I had spent many a narcissistic hour before the mirror examining each feature and despairing of all of them. Particularly my nose. I would have given anything for a turned up nose. 'But sometimes I forget . . .' I gulped some coke. My voice had begun wavering.

'More foolishness. There's nothing wrong with your face. It's a good, strong Venetian one. I can easily show you that. It's no use feeling inferior to anyone. Besides you could pick up their . . . polish.'

'How?'

'Well,' you laughed, 'I wouldn't know. But I could think of someone who would — if you're interested. Someone who could help you. To work on the small details. Let's see . . .' You hesitated only for a second. 'Elena. Of course! She'll know what's to be done. Do you remember Elena?'

Who could forget Elena? I hadn't seen her since I'd moved to Canada and had seen her rarely enough before, but her image, luminous, intense, had stuck with me. 'Elena,' I knew even at fourteen, 'has never had to worry about small details — what lipstick, what length of hair. Never.'

'Perhaps, but she'll still know how to help you. You can depend on it.'

Tired from two late nights, I slept late the next morning. And when I did wake up I felt odd: my head curiously light, my body heavy, drugged. I was edging my way down the long corridor to the kitchen when, in the archway that divided the two, you and Elena suddenly appeared. Elena seemed to be trying to evade you. She was laughing. You caught her against the wall, one arm by her head, your body blocking hers. The sun from the kitchen windows shone like a spotlight, emphasizing her golden hair, white tennis clothes, and the expression, the concentration of your blue, blue eyes. I stood still, an unwitting audience in the dark hall. You were teasing her — about beating her on the courts I think, joking about the inconsistency of women. She answered sharply, alternately aggressive and coy. I was surprised with how often, over the years, the scene of the two of you in that morning sun replayed itself in my mind. Maybe it was because, although your voice and your words were the usual, your body betrayed a Marco I had never seen before, with all the coolness and detachment gone.

I knew as I stood and watched that I was seeing what I had not been able to see before. Not love, but the possibility of what could be between a man and a woman. You pushed back a strand of her hair and I felt the touch. She laid her hand on your arm and my arm felt her cool fingers.

Yet, even then, I could see that while you were totally there, she was not. Part of her was holding herself in reserve, amused but not engaged.

You moved back, freeing her, but you barely looked at me. 'Elena's been waiting.'

Elena fell into step beside me so we entered the kitchen and crossed over to the table together. 'Nice to see you again, Bianca.' I responded with a grunt. 'Marco says that you'd like some advice. I don't have any time today. A tennis game on the Lido.'

'A very important game. She has to put

another one of her wretched admirers into his place. Poor man.' They exchanged a smiling glance.

'Marco, stop it! Shall we fix another day?'

I was gathering my breakfast together, not looking at her. 'I didn't expect to see you so soon.' Though, of course, you had called her immediately. It had all been a handy excuse for you to see her.

'How about tomorrow evening? At my house?' Elena had draped herself on the chair opposite mine. 'I have a couple of hours. Oh and I could make an appointment with my hairdresser for the next day, if that's all right?'

'No,' I buried my face for a long moment in my coffee bowl. 'I've changed my mind.'

You were looking irritated. 'You said . . .'

'I don't want to be polished. I want my rough edges. I'm attached to them. Why should I try to be what I'm not?'

'I thought you weren't sure what you were?' Irritation was giving way to amusement.

I expected Elena to shrug her trim shoulders and withdraw. She surprised me. 'I do understand you. I agree. But it never hurts to learn how to play the game well before re-jecting it. Then you function from a position of strength. Come tomorrow evening.' She was hard to resist. She had a rare talent for making the subject of her attention feel truly under-stood, appreciated. It was a talent that sprang,

I suspect, from the intensity of her gaze, from the quickness, the sensitivity of her response.

'Elena's really something,' I said to you after we had fixed a time and she had gone.

'Yes.'

I knew it would be wiser to leave it at that, but I couldn't. 'But it won't work out with you two.'

'What on earth are you talking about?'

'You could make yourself a habit, but not more. She'll never feel as you do.'

'Riddles. Are we playing riddles?'

'Marco!'

You smiled, tweaked my nose. You knew, but only on a level far from the surface, far from light. Elena shifted constantly, but you believed eventually she must settle, must come to rest. Then she would be at hand.

Her bedroom, that evening I visited, was sparse, cell-like. The walls were bare except for two shelves. One held books, the other a record player and a few records. Her bed was narrow and covered with a tattered spread. The only profusion lay on the top of her dressing table — bottles, tubes, little boxes, sticks, a red silk rose, a large mirror lined with light bulbs to simulate three kinds of light.

'Far out. Do you use all this stuff?'

Elena laughed. 'Rarely.' She guided me onto a small stool and pulled up the only other chair, a straight-backed one, for herself. Our faces were reflected side by side in the mirror:

a depressing sight. 'I wanted to be a singer. This was part of the package.'

'Wanted?'

'Actually,' she was sifting through the containers, 'I wanted to be a star. I thought it would resolve everything. So I went off to Cinecittà, face and voice in hand.'

'But you came back?'

She was cleaning my face with lotion. 'Umm. It took me a year or so to realize how deadly it was. Turning myself into a little package. All tied up in glittery string. Love me. Love me. Buy me. Buy me.' She was making up the right side of my face, bracketing her story with precise instructions on the application of foundation and eye shadow. 'Not that my voice was exceptional. Pleasant would be the more accurate term. But, you see, I'd been brought up to rely on how I looked. Thought it would bring me what I needed. What lies! It could bring only what I didn't need. Besides, pretty faces are so common that they're worth less than a *lira*.'

'I don't know.' I was trying to repeat her work on my right side on my left. My fingers were heavier than hers, less subtle. She leaned over and blotted out with regularity. 'I'm sorry I was so stubborn yesterday.'

'Bianca, you should realize by now that I understood perfectly.'

'Well, I'm just mixed up about it all. It's all the nuns' fault.'

'The nuns! Dreaded ravens.'

'They're so down on men and . . . you know.'

'Certainly. Men are beasts and the flesh is dirt, all that.'

'Yes. But they are also always telling us to be feminine. Not to raise our voices, not to think of a career. "Soft, sweet and pleasing," Mother Geneviève says. Feminine. It's the most used word around St. Mary's Girls. Feminine. Yuck. They can have it.'

'So they warn you of the butcher while preparing you for the slaughter.'

'You do understand. So why all this gunk? Why cover up what you are, what you believe, with this paint?'

'We can all use a mask from time to time.' Elena smiled at me. 'You're young yet. You'll see.' She began speaking of the eighteenth-century *carnevale*, of the masks and the dominoes that obliterated personal, class, and sometimes even sexual differences. 'Freedom,' her voice was lowered to a whisper. 'Can you imagine?'

Elena continued to surprise me in her openness, her patience, her kindness. The next day she took me shopping, to her hairdresser and, as a final treat, to Florian's for coffee and ice cream.

'I never thought I would sit here. It's so expensive. And touristy.'

Elena raised her demitasse to me. 'In

honour of your transformation.' Though I wasn't actually transformed. I hadn't become her. There was an improvement, certainly. The hairdresser had straightened my hair into a smooth cap. The makeup brought out, deepened, my features. I felt cocky and not a bit compromised. I didn't even mind that the glance of each passing male was drawn to her, never me.

'Extremist. Brigadist,' your mother called Elena in one letter, besides other less polite names. Aunt Elsa wrote to tell how shocked and totally surprised the family was that Elena had involved you and that you had let yourself be involved. I couldn't understand the surprise. Didn't they remember how you looked at her? They both added, however, perhaps from the remnants of an old loyalty, that Elena must have been duped, drugged into cooperation. 'She was such a sweet girl.'

She was. We sat in the late afternoon sun watching the pigeons and the people. Giggling together as if we were both fourteen. Extreme? The only extreme I saw was the excess of her beauty, her sensitivity. But I see the pattern of Elena's and my brief relationship as a reflection of all her other relationships. Nothing that I heard later disputed this. All the gossip about her search through psychotherapy, student politics, feminism, 'busily seeking with a continual change', did not disclose me another design. She was always the strong one, the wise one; we fed off her excess. And she, when weak, when vulnerable, turned not to those to whom she gave but to theories, philosophies. She could not change the pattern, so she destroyed it. '*Noli me tangere.* Do not touch me. I am no longer what I was.'

That afternoon, speaking to me of her favourites, Bessie Smith and Billie Holiday, Elena said, 'It's not the way — the end of that journey can only be death.' She chose another journey. At the end, death waits, just as surely. And yet she rushes, arms outstretched. Soon, soon she will arrive. She will be found neatly laid out on her narrow childhood bed, a journal cataloguing regrets under her pillow, an empty bottle of pills by her hand. Or sprawled on a city street mangled by a hail of police bullets. I wish her at least that. A dramatic, public end — still under the protection of her system of belief, still with her new companions, still not what she was. Fused by the flame of action, the flame fuelled of our needs, into a metallic ikon. Saint of backrooms, of mimeographed manifestos, of clandestine meetings. Martyr, not victim.

***

In the last two weeks of my summer, you took that series of pictures you were to call 'Venetian Studies'. All over the city we walked; I helping you carry the lenses, the tripod. You always took your time about taking the picture, checking different angles, different filters. But I was never bored. For as you carefully thought, looked and adjusted, you would explain a detail of the architecture or tell me a story connected to a particular spot or house. 'This lion dates from the sixth century B.C. It was taken from Delos when Corfu was captured.' 'These three statues are supposed to be Arabian merchants, which is why . . .' You made me notice all that I habitually glanced over. And though you posed me for the camera, my concentration was so caught that I stayed relaxed, natural.

Later, when you showed me the pictures I appeared in, I was amazed. You said, 'You see, Bianca, you see how you are beautiful.' And the girl in those pictures was. I never looked like that before or again. Not even in the many pictures you were to take of me in the following years. But I was not fooled. I knew it was art, not reality. Still, you had given me a precious gift. A refinement, an abstraction of the basic me. 'I wanted you to see,' you said.

Spread on the desk in front of me I have a few small prints of those pictures. I flip through them. They make me a little uneasy. A man I was involved with had one of them blown up, not to the size you exhibited but to larger-than-life size. He hung it on his wall. It haunted me particularly when he and I made love. I initiated complicated positions just so I didn't have to see that image of me gazing down over his shoulder. He refused to take it down. He was like that; he wrote sentimental poetry. Beside those pictures I lay out a photo snapped by a sidewalk cameraman. It is the only one I have of you and me. We are hurrying to the *Merchant of Venice*, caught in mid-stride. I am dowdy, with tight curls; your nose looks particularly large, your cheeks sunken. There is a large space between us and our expressions; our looks are so divergent. We do not seem to be together at all. Rather, we seem two strangers, caught in the same frame by chance.

Finally, I lay out a picture taken when I was eight, just before my family emigrated. I am sitting at a table, behind an elaborately decorated birthday cake. But my round-cheeked face is turned so that I'm gazing up at Elena. She is standing behind me, her hands resting on my shoulders. She is laughing into the camera.

She dazzles me still.

XIV

The ancient stones of Venice had to be there, submerged by the green slimy water but still solid, supporting, to be counted on. Yet, each step took an act of faith, for each step was a step off, a step into. He moved more deliberately than was necessary, keeping close to the side of buildings, watching his rubber-booted legs as they plunged in, feeling distinctly each meeting of stone and foot. In the big flood of 1966, he had taken a sequence of photographs that had won him some prizes both in Italy and Sweden. He had deliberately overexposed the prints so that the water came out as a white blank expanse that emphasized the blackness of the long hurrying figures and their shattered reflections. It was the way he had viewed his body and, by extension, man's state then; isolated but with a clarity and importance in that isolation. His lone figures seemed to walk on the water. They did not edge. They did not hesitate. If he took pictures today, he would make them hazy, studies in different shades of grey.

The sky, choked with clouds, had a heavy, stifling quality. The water was already dropping; the sludge mark, testifying to the highest point of the flood, was quite visible. Still, the rain began again. First softly, an almost-warm caress to his face; but gradually harder, needling. He opened his umbrella at a dry spot at the top of a bridge. Just a few feet away, down the other side, was a trail of *passarelle*. All through the winter months, the wooden boards and metal frames lay stacked in corners of the *campi* or pushed up against the walls of the *viale*. As soon as the water began to rise, they were set up to form a path that wound through and around the entire city.

There were not many people about. Just ahead of him, a fat woman in a mink coat was moving ponderously, boards creaking loudly. When she glanced over her shoulder, Marco recognized her as one of the fish sellers on the Rialto. A serious-faced man was coming towards him. Both he and the man dropped their umbrellas to opposite sides and side-stepped past each other. Marco felt as if they were part of a strictly patterned dance occurring all over the city on the stage of the *passarelle*. Indeed, a bit farther on, he came upon a little boy of about eight, sitting, swishing his legs through the water, watching two little girls who stood arms around each other, giggling and singing 'Singing in the Rain'. Their English was heavily accented. 'Singing in the Rain.' One attempted a dance step and nearly fell off.

Here the way to his brother's branched off

from the path. He lowered himself back into the dark flood. The giggles followed him. 'No. No. Sing*ing* . . . Sing*ing*.' He edged his way around the corner, past the Padovani café where several patrons were contentedly sitting at tables, their legs resting on chairs. Another corner and he was on the final stretch. In his eagerness to be again on the dry and solid, he quickened his step. Instantly, his foot slipped. He struggled for balance, one knee, one umbrella-less hand, plunged into the viscous water. He managed to right himself, to avoid falling, but he still shuddered at the idea that the filth, the foulness of centuries, might have touched his face, stained his lips, insinuated itself into his mouth.

Regaining his calm, he looked up to an odd sight at the end of the *fondamento,* a man with someone holding an umbrella perched on his shoulders. A bit closer, Marco realized it was Tarquinio, tilted forward like some top-heavy sailing boat, and Lea, her face streaming with tears.

'I was just coming to your house.'

'It's her mother. We're going to the hospital.' Tarquinio's face was neutral as if the situation were an everyday one.

'God, I'm very sorry. Can I do anything?'

Tarquinio shook his head. 'It would happen today of all days. Just my luck . . .'

'What happened? Was it another stroke, Lea?' She did not answer. She did not even look at Marco. The tears kept rolling down her cheek, off her jaw. Her normally small, fine-featured face was swollen, splotched purply-red. Her mouth twisted and trembled. Yet, she held the umbrella steadily enough, managing to keep off that minute portion of the wetness.

'Another one.' Tarquinio was already moving on, his face turned up to Lea. 'Can't you hold yourself up a bit more. This is very difficult . . . I should change my name to Christopher,' he called back to his brother.

Marco had not expected to discuss the past night with Tarquinio. Still, he realized as he mounted the stairs, he had counted on talking to him and, maybe in a general way, touching on a bit of it. It would have been an outlet of sorts. Marco was not in the habit of going to his brother for either advice or sympathy, but still he looked to Tarquinio as an example. From infancy on, he had been aware that in so many things his brother had already crossed the river, already shown the way, even if only negatively. Tarquinio's experience with emigration, with lack of work had helped Marco decide to go back to school and to go on to university. 'You were smart,' his brother often said to him. 'You're not stuck, forever the mule hauling loads, like me. If I had your education, your salary, your job . . .'

And, Marco thought as he was let in the door and began pulling off his boots, if I had your wife, your daughters. Barbara, curled up on the sofa, turned away from the TV film she was watching to blow him a kiss. '*Ciao, Zio.*' Patrizia, emerging from the bathroom, bespectacled, hair in rollers, made a sleepy face at him.

'It's Saturday. Why isn't everyone in bed?'

'Too crowded. Mine's packed full of Brigadists.'

'For sure.'

'Patrizia would sleep all day if we let her.' This came from Aunt Elsa who had let him in. 'Her teachers are on strike again.'

'Don't worry. I didn't forget. Wish I could.'

Elsa ushered Marco into the kitchen. 'You're lucky. There is still some hot tea. It will take the chill off. It's terrible out there. It gets worse and worse.'

'How serious is the stroke?' Elsa passed him a plate of *amaretti* to go with the tea.

'Oh, it's serious all right.' She was back at the sink, scrubbing the cups with particular vigour. 'Close to the end, they say. What can you expect with the kind of life she's lived? Never controlled herself in anything. So fat and she knew something was wrong. But she never would go to the doctor. Didn't trust them, she said. You know those *Chioggiote*. So, you saw Lea? You saw the state she was in? She could barely stand. For once, I must say, I agree with your mother. She phoned just before they left. Your mother told her to stop overreacting. She came out and said, "What are you going on about — it's not as if your mother ever did much for you — especially after your father took off to Australia!' Just like that she said it. And she's right. That woman just stuck Lea in the convent school. She was only six. And she left her there. Carried on with her "private life". And quite a life it was, I can tell you. I saw the men going in and out at all hours. I know . . . And now Lea's acting as if she's losing the best mother in the world. Of course, maybe your mother shouldn't have said anything today, seeing the state she was in.'

'I would have thought not.'

'Lea does have weak nerves.'

Down the hall, the phone rang. Marco's hand flicked out, hitting his cup and almost upsetting it. 'Your nerves aren't in the best shape either,' Elsa managed to comment on her way out.

Marco let the tea-dipped biscuit dissolve in his mouth, savouring the almond-flavoured sweetness. Swallowing was more difficult. His stomach had erected a barrier halfway down his throat. For aid, he took a mouthful of tea. It was warm to his mouth, but when it hit his stomach, it revealed itself as burning hot.

About a year ago, on another rainy day, he had sat at this table, drinking tea with Lea. That day she was not so much nervous as awkward. Her hands fluttered about more than normally. Her dark, round-eyed gaze kept flickering away from him, fixing on the tablecloth, her hands.

He knew she had been asked by Paola to talk to him. The situation between him and his wife had degenerated to the point of his looking for an available sublet. With a certain delicacy Lea offered all the usual clichés of family and responsibility. Marco was tempted to cut her off. It would have been easy: a joke, an insistence on his side, or even a gentle 'pulling rank', but he made himself listen and reply. For Lea's urging for a new try, a new commitment, was Paola's proud method of reaching out, of saying 'Let us begin again.'

Flushed with the easy success, Lea grew more expansive. The flutters became broad sweeping gestures, the prepared speech turned to chatter. Marco should know. 'No one gets exactly what he wants.' Everyone has problems. Why, she herself wondered at times, wasn't there more? But one had to try for what was possible. And, only pausing to pour more tea, she began recounting the story of the family whose windows faced theirs across the *calle.*

The husband, Signor Bevilacqua, was a reserved man even before the tragedy. He was well-respected around the neighbourhood. He had a dignified, polite manner that went with his prematurely greying hair and his management job at the Casino. He seemed dedicated to his wife and daughter. He often carried bouquets of flowers or large packages from the toy store. He was punctual and orderly. The way his expensive coat fit snugly over his shoulders, the way he kept his hair short and brushed back, his shoes shiny and polished, it all showed how he liked to have things just right.

The wife, Signora Marisa, was a different story. She did not command respect even before she began to change. In the shops she was too familiar: too quick to turn a remark into a joke and too quick to complain, to insist on her rights. She lacked the authority, the dignity a serious married woman was expected to have. Walking with her daughter, she was liable, without warning, to break into hopscotch or chant a song. A hike of her skirt and away she went. And her laugh! It was totally unrestrained. She let it loose at the oddest times: while reading a newspaper headline at the kiosk or standing in line, eavesdropping at the milk store.

Marco had known Marisa slightly in high school and had, in fact, admired 'from afar'. She was one of the *figlie di Papa*, a privileged one, and the rigid class structure of a high school in the late fifties permitted no more. But he recalled and argued for her as high-spirited and quick-witted rather than sharp-tongued and silly.

The change had come when her daughter was around four. The Signora abandoned her suits and silk blouses for long velvet skirts, beribboned tops, and antique nighties that she wore as dresses. She began frequenting galleries instead of hairdressers, buying books instead of makeup. She had discovered art and artists — one in particular. They were seen on the *vaporetto*, at Florian's, at the Pesaro, always talking intently. Her husband did not seem to react. He was still punctual, even when she wasn't there. Only his step on the *calle* seemed different, more hurried.

It was not understood, at first, why the Signora took up with the young bride who lived in the apartment above her. Chiara was certainly an unusually beautiful girl, 'a pleasure to watch walk by', the cronies of Padovani bar pronounced; with the light green eyes, translucent skin, and high cheekbones that you find in those towns at the base of the Dolomites. Chiara still went about, like a schoolgirl, in tight jeans, long tee-shirts, and her hair in a braid hung down her back. And, like a schoolgirl, she had a passion for late sixties American music, which she played loudly as she did housework and which, since she usually kept the shutters and the windows open, reverberated down the *calle*.

With the difference in age, class, and interests, it was hard to see Chiara as Signora Marisa's 'dear friend', but there it was. 'I was envious of them,' Lea said, 'I would watch them sitting on the *terrazza*, the one opposite Patrizia's room, smoking, laughing. I thought, why her and not me?' When the summer came, they went every day to the Lido together. The Signora had a *capanna* on the Excelsior beach.

It was only gradually that the friendship became comprehensible. Chiara, her thick hair loose, her green eyes high-lighted by shadow, all under Signora Marisa's direction, was being offered. The Signora would ask her to help by doing some ironing, some babysitting. Then Marisa would have a pressing appointment and her husband would be there. No one was surprised when Bevilacqua took the exquisite gift his wife was tempting him with. But the intensity of the taking — that was surprising. He came back every day at noon, not home but to Chiara's apartment. Everyone noticed: her shutters closed in the middle of the day, and when later she opened them again, her joyous smile. His face relaxed, opened. His smile became quick, ever-ready. He took to greeting effusively all the people he had ignored for the last eight years. In Chiara the signs were most noticeable in her body; fuller breasts and hips, a new way of walking, as if she enjoyed every step.

Did her husband suspect anything? He was a thin, bespectacled young man, with a lowly clerical job, but he was ambitious and made it clear to all the other patrons of Padovani's café that he intended to move up quickly. Perhaps he was too blinded by his future to see. (He certainly worked longer hours than were necessary.) Or perhaps he didn't want to see. Like his rival, he gave the impression that he wanted everything to be in order. Unlike his rival, he did not confine this impulse to himself and his actions, but imposed it on Chiara. From the first days that they moved into the apartment, he was noted for his bursts of anger, emerging so ridiculously from his narrow frame, his mild face. In spite of the suddenness and fury of his tirades, he did not inspire fear, or even dislike — simply embarrassment. It was inappropriate for him to berate his wife in the *campo* or toss plates of food out of the window.

Otherwise, he was likeable enough, obsessed with soccer in the winter and tennis in the summer, concerned with meeting the right people, the useful people, who were 'connections' to where he wanted to go. Indeed, though a newcomer, he fit right into the café gang. They all knew what it was like to be on the lowest rung. They all enjoyed his carefully memorized jokes, his tales of how he bested his supervisors or how he was being done in by his landlady. They took him to soccer games with them and included him in their long nights of political arguing over red wine. Strangely, in these discussions he was the calmest, the most soft-spoken.

When Chiara's affair came to the attention of the gang, it took them five minutes to decide that he had to be told. Was it protection of one of their own? Not entirely. He was still too new to Venice not to suspect a relish, a mali-

cious enjoyment in telling a man he is a cuck-
old. 'Look to your wife.'

'I heard a few crashes and their voices were
raised,' Lea said, 'but it wasn't so extraordi-
nary. When Chiara closed the shutters, I
thought — there — they'll make it up in bed.
They're young, they'll work it out.'

Who called the police? Not known, but
when they arrived they found a gas-filled apart-
ment and both of them dead. They lay on their
wide matrimonial bed in what seemed a final
embrace. Only a closer look showed that he
had held her down, that she had struggled,
that his hands were still clamped around her
bruised wrists.

Who told Signora Marisa? Also not known,
but when her husband reached the *calle* that
noon, she was standing on their *terrazza* wait-
ing in the rain. She didn't seem to notice how
wet she was, how her hair was plastered to her
head and how the tears ran down her cheeks.

'She's dead,' she called to him.

'Sonia?' (Their daughter.)

'Chiara. Both of them. She and her
husband. Gassed.' And he fainted, right there
on the wet stones.

Signora Marisa and Sonia moved out even
before the divorce came through. She and her
new artist husband have made a name as social
leaders in the gallery set. Bevilacqua remains
alone. Year after year. He brings his daughter
home once a week. When it's nice, they have

lunch on the *terrazza*. You can hear them laugh together, so at least he has that. And every summer, he takes a *capanna* next to the one of his ex-wife.

From the degree of detail Lea gave while telling this story, from the silence she sank into when she finished, Marco could see behind his sister-in-law's habitual mask, could feel her sense of loss. 'No one gets exactly what he wants,' she had said, and he had wanted to ask her what she wanted, but the question seemed impertinent. Besides, he should know how general, how pervasive the sense of loss could become and how deep and hidden the roots. 'What are you thinking of?' Marco turned away from the window to the voice. His bland response dried in his throat. A lovely, high-cheekboned girl, with one braid hanging over her shoulder, stood by the stove. The young wife of Lea's story, here before him. His tongue almost pronounced the syllables Chiara. 'You looked so lost in thought. Lots on your mind I expect.'

'Oh, Patrizia . . . You are growing up. I almost didn't recognize you . . .'

'What? Didn't recognize me? You are in a daze. You've seen me in contacts before . . . You saw me last night.'

'Of course . . . I was thinking of something else.'

'Umm. Wish I could.' She was heating up some *caffè e latte*. 'Aunt Elsa, you'll be happy to hear, is on the phone to one of her friends bad-mouthing my mother.'

'Surely, today of all days . . .'

'She is. And it bugs me. It really bugs me. Mum doesn't need it.' Patrizia carried her cup to the table and drew up a chair peculiarly close to Marco's.

'It is a type of concern. She hates to see your mother so distressed.' Now that she was beside him, Marco could see that she had layered on the paint again.

'Don't let's talk about this family.' Patrizia cocked her head at a coquettish angle. 'I don't want to hear anything more. I want to hear about what's on your mind.' Her smile was sly; her eyes held his.

He should have known that she had reached that stage. Her anxiety was visibly weighing her down, effecting the turn away from childhood. Marco roused himself from his chair and crossed over to the window. 'I was thinking of a story your mother told me once about the people who lived across the way. I guess it happened a few years ago.'

'Mum told you about that! I'm surprised.' Patrizia was relaxing back into girlhood.

'Why? You seem to know the tale.'

'Of course. Hard not to. But Dad forbade Mum to tell anyone. Even referring to it. I overheard him . . . He was MAD.'

'Now you surprise me.' He could not imagine it. His brother would not act so.

'Oh, I'm full of surprises.' She was at it again.

Marco squelched her with a frown. 'I suppose Tarquinio would be against gossip.'

Patrizia laughed. 'Hardly. He just doesn't want Mum looking out at that apartment. It bothers him. Just like he doesn't want her to smile at the fish seller or to stop in a bar for a coffee. And on and on.' (Were the deep roots, the flourishing tree that he accepted as Tarquinio an illusion?)

For once, Marco was pleased to see Elsa enter the room. Patrizia went on, but she was forced to change gears. She began muttering about families and repression, about hypocrisy and convention. Elsa, meanwhile, began nattering on about the dreadful film Barbara was watching. The two voices pricked and prodded him. 'I don't know what the world's coming to . . .'

'My friends and I, we talk — we have this dream of a perfect place, of a perfect community. Free, innocent.'

'I was nearly sick. Right there. Breast out, exposed. In the morning yet.'

'A place based on love and sharing. Why can't people . . .'

Marco stood by the kitchen window and stared across at the shutters of that opposite apartment and waited for the time to come for him to go to the *Accademia*, waited for his wife and son to return. And while the voices droned on, while the moments inched by, he saw Lea's distorted face under the umbrella, crying for her mother who was not a mother, he saw Tarquinio stopping and starting, shifting his shoulders as he carried his wife high above the murky waters. Unease, uncertainty was everywhere. And suddenly, Marco was no longer calm in his empathetic reverie. His fears pressed for attention. Looking down the narrow street reminded him now only of his own street and of how many eyes might have noticed his nocturnal visitors.

Afternoon

XV

The galleries were empty. Room after room unfolded themselves to him — his private preserve. Even when he came to see a particular picture, he would meander, pause at a few favourites — Giorgione's *Tempesta*, Carpaccio's St. Ursula series. But this unlikely morning, when each painting seemed to hang for his eyes, he could not stop. The message he was to deliver, the words he must utter, shimmered in an insulating haze around him. His steps were soundless on the grey carpet, but his way was highlighted by the skylights and the track lamps against the blur of the pictures.

As he approached the early Renaissance rooms, he found a covey of Australian tourists. Their faces were turned to the paintings, but they were loudly congratulating themselves on their intrepidness and cleverness in having found the gallery open. Marco edged past — they were half-blocking the doorway — into the long room where he knew a few of the Bellinis to be. Giovanni Bellini. Was this the gallery? There was *Sacred Conversations*, the colours glowing at him. But could this be called the Bellini room? Had Piero even meant

Giovanni, or was it Jacopo or Gentile? How would it be judged if he missed the man? Would 'I wasn't sure where you meant' serve? Quiet. Piero would not be random in his choice. There must be a thread of reasons, however fine. Sacred Conversations. No, that implied a delicate irony inimical to Piero's style. It must be something by Gentile, that acute observer of external rather than spiritual realities. The Bellini room. Of course, Room XX, the paintings commissioned by the School of St. John the Evangelist. Only two of the three paintings were by Gentile, but that still made it more of a Bellini room than where he was, which had three Giovanni's out of twenty.

And, in fact, when he reached Room XX, he realized that from a practical — never mind a symbolical — point of view, this must be the designated meeting place. It was off the main tour path and small in comparison to most of the galleries. Sitting on the bench, Marco could see both doorways, yet seemed to be intent on observing those tremendous paintings.

Eleven twenty-seven. At least he was at the correct place at the correct time. He leaned back, clasped his hands around his knees and let his eyes focus on the Bellinis. In the first, *The Procession of the True Cross*, he saw only the glowing gold, the touches of red, the balance and symmetry of the figures, but when he shifted to *The Miracle of the True Cross*, the size, the intensity, the vitality of the picture began to take him up. He had always had a weakness for Gentile, though his works, unlike those of his greater, more successful father, brother, or brother-in-law, evoked no dreams, no abandon. Gentile Bellini had painted a crystallization of the external reality of his age — Venice of the fifteenth century — and that was dream, that was 'other', enough.

Marco knew that the picture had been painted as a type of medieval public relations. The leader (soon to be elected *Doge*) of the charitable brotherhood that had commissioned the painting, was portrayed as miraculously discovering and rescuing the Holy Cross from the canal where it had fallen on a previous procession. But the leader by no means dominated the picture. He was no larger, no more individually done, than the row of praying women, the group of impassive officials, the throng of monks on the bridge, each holding his candlestick at a different angle. It was a portrait of the Venetian people at their best, united in purpose, in industriousness, in confidence, in belief; the sense of community, of collaboration, implicit. 'A commercial people who lived solely for gain.' Certainly, but what they created with that gain. Over one thousand years of glory, the longest republic the world has seen, 'The eldest child of liberty.' Until Napoleon, they bowed to no one, conqueror, pope, or dictator. What they created. Not only the palaces and the *campi,* not only an excess of art and music, but an elaborate machine of government beyond the 'irrationality of man'. The nobility ruled and yet there were no titles; family was essential, yet boasting of one's forefathers brought a fine. Venice: well might they look confident.

'I've always wondered about that black man,' the voice was close to his right ear. A young man, black coat, red plaid shirt, had sat on the bench beside him. 'The figure on the right, peering down into the water. He doesn't fit. Why is he almost naked?' The man's hands were white and doughy. His face round, the features curiously flat. His moustache was so thin, it looked drawn on. His hair, however, was profuse: tight black curls reaching his shoulders.

'I suppose he's a servant,' Marco finally managed.

'But what is he doing? Is he going to jump in or is he still looking for the cross, not realizing they've got it already? Dumb-like.'

'I never thought about it.'

'Well. I have. He must have been a slave. He looks like one. Did they have many slaves? Do you know?' He would pause slightly after each question, his dark flat eyes searching Marco's face as if he alone had the answer.

'I don't think they did. Not so late.'

'I wish I knew more history . . . what *is* that man doing there?'

'Maybe it was a private little joke of the artist's. They do that.'

'What about the men in the canal? They're like corpses floating there.'

This was drawing out far too long. 'Bellini probably wanted the connotation of resurrection. The painting is called *The Miracle of the Cross*.'

'Rebirth in the canals of Venice. Descending and rising from the muck.'

'It was a different era from ours, an era of faith and confidence.'

The man's eyes were still, intent. 'And now?'

Marco casually gazed around the room through the two doorways. 'Now is the time of action.'

The man turned back to the painting, 'A time of terrible beauty.'

Who thought up these lines? Marco stifled the urge to say that he could see the terribleness all right but not much of the beauty; transformation, that was what was lacking. He stuck to the script. 'If the water is down, the demonstration begins at 16:00.'

The young man turned to Marco again. 'I never miss them — demonstrations, I mean.' He laughed, his flat face crinkling up, like a picture on rumpled paper, his big body shaking flaccidly as he stood up. 'Take care of yourself.'

What could be the appropriate reply to

that? You too, when the young man so obviously didn't.

The young man, now standing between Marco and *The Miracle of the Cross*, leaned over, bending from the waist so that his nose almost touched Marco's. 'The beasts are awakening.' He pulled back, straightened, but he left behind an unwanted gift, the disquieting odour of musty clothes and stale patchouli.

It clung — that smell — a brown gas tainting the air. It clung through several hours, all the way to Piazzale Roma where, finally, it was overwhelmed by the foulness of car and bus exhaust. The stink of the real world. Strange how often he found himself thinking that; each time he crossed the wooden bridge to Piazzale Roma he saw himself as crossing into the real world, crossing ill-equipped, 'a fish out of water'.

In fact, as he stood on the sidewalk, away from the curb, waiting for the 3:05 from Padova, a Fiat 500 which had been aggressively weaving its way through the congested traffic halted momentarily by a bus, paused, revved its little motor and humped its way onto the sidewalk. Marco froze, unable to quite believe in this car merrily speeding towards him. Incongruously, the driver was a large-headed, serious-faced, middle-aged man. The two other men waiting for the bus, in their scramble to get out of the way, had to attach themselves to the side of the depot. Just in time, Marco, feeling a bit too ridiculous, jumped sideways and flattened himself against the concrete and glass.

All of which was why he did not notice the Padova bus pull in. He looked up from brushing his clothes off and saw Paola and Francesco on the sidewalk about two bus lengths away. His heart, already agitated, took off, his pulse pounding in his forehead. How they stood out from the everydayness, the sheer normality of the other passengers. Paola had over-dressed Francesco, as she always did in winter on the few occasions when he was allowed out. A beige and brown down-filled ski suit encased his short, pudgy body, a thick beige scarf swaddled his throat, but it was the balaclava, covering all but his puffy mouth and eyes that contributed most to his extraordinary appearance. Francesco was fidgeting restlessly, hopping on one leg and then the other, flapping his stiff-suited arms in and out — like some mechanical space monster.

And Paola. She was dressed and stood discreetly enough, but the face she turned to Marco as he started toward her was not at all her usual, composed face; it was both tight and puffy, both distracted and obsessed, but above all, it was desperate.

Yet, as he moved closer, the desperation seemed to recede so that when he stood before her he suspected what he had seen had only been a trick of sight. In greeting, he let his hand brush her cheek where those deep lines had appeared. But Paola pulled back, instinctively it seemed, her eyes not meeting his but roving over the crowd. Francesco was grunting, pulling on Marco's coat. The father bent to the son.

XVI

Marco carried Francesco all the way home. Although the water had dropped considerably, he had brought boots for both Paola and the boy. Still Paola insisted that Francesco should not walk. Marco, already irritated by the way she had overdressed Francesco, made a comment about her overprotectiveness. 'It's not fair to him; it's like keeping him in cotton batting. He has a limited enough life as it is, but you cut off the little contact he could have with the world.' He knew as soon as the words were out that it was the wrong time to say them. All of the frustration Paola had experienced in Padova erupted in anger against him. So they walked together over the bridges, through the puddles: Paola railing, her voice sometimes choking, Marco weaving a bit from the weight of his child.

The clouds had cleared. The water that remained in the *fondamenti* and the *campi* was just at the right level, with the afternoon sun shining, to mirror the surrounding buildings. Venice doubled and the three of them caught on the fulcrum of the doubleness — walking parody of the happy, reunited family.

Francesco kept his face pressed to Marco's neck; his imprecise tongue struggled to pronounce the syllables. 'Pa-Pa.'

'*Caro mio.*' Marco was struggling himself, but to readjust the boy to a more comfortable position.

'I will cut him off. I'll do anything I have to do. Don't you remember what happened when he got chicken pox? Two weeks in the hospital. You would insist on his going to his cousin's party. Two weeks. He couldn't breathe. Don't you remember? I won't go through that again. Never again.' (Though Paola knew — they both knew — she would and worse. That was what the trip to Padova was about.)

Fortunately, their apartment was not far from Piazzale Roma. Marco's arms had just hit the trembling stage when they reached their building. He put Francesco down and massaged them before trying the stairs. He did not look at Paola. He could imagine her facial expression. Suddenly, as if the pressure of his fingers on his tweed jacket had broken a secret scent vial, the young man's smell was back, mustier and staler than ever. Marco took a step away from his wife and child. He waited for Paola's comment. She was always fastidious, but she made none.

Again, the smell stuck to him; even more pervasively, it seemed, than before. For it was not only on him. Stepping into the apartment, he found it already there, a noxious cloud lying in wait. Paola still seemed oblivious. She was ahead of him, bracelets jangling, leading Francesco down the hall, speaking in the gentle voice she reserved for the boy. Francesco was in obvious need of a nap; otherwise he wouldn't have been so acquiescent in being carried so far. Paola managed to have him undressed and lying in his bed in a couple of minutes.

'This all has been hard on him. Exhausting,' she said to Marco as she took off her own coat. 'He was starting to go a bit blue around the mouth.'

'Yes, I saw that.'

'You noticed too.' Her glance at Marco was almost surprised. 'I have to put my things away.' She smoothed her dark sweater over her hips, checked her hair in the hall mirror. 'Come and we'll talk.'

Marco carried the small suitcase into their bedroom and laid it on the bed. She unzipped it and began unpacking. Sitting on the left corner of the bed (where, a few hours before, Elena had sat and smiled at him), he watched her. 'Tell me. I know, but tell me.'

The specialists had all seen him. The experts of heart, of retardation, of special learning, of genetics; cold-eyed, they had tested, weighed, observed, analysed, and judged. The condition of his heart could mean one year, two years. Tomorrow. Paola was sitting with her back to him at her dressing table replacing her tubes of makeup, her bracelets, and her necklaces into the drawer. Her head was bent, her dark smooth hair had fallen forward so he could not see most of her face in the reflection the mirror threw back to him. But her prominent green eyes shone through the wisps of hair. His own face in the mirror was ridiculous: bulbous nose, sunken cheeks — a comedy mask, worse, a gargoyle. There was an operation that could extend the child's life, but it was complicated, expensive, and, the experts argued, inappropriate.

'I knew it.' Marco stood behind her, his hand resting on her shoulders.

'I won't accept it. There are other doctors. Even if we have to go to Houston. There are miracle workers there.' Their eyes met in the mirror. Paola's had a new expression, glazed. 'Or if we have to — make them change their mind. Inappropriate. How dare they! I've been doing a lot of thinking. I've decided.'

His ugly face was wavering, as if in preparation for a more horrendous metamorphosis. Instead, black spots appeared, spread, joined up, blanking him inside and out.

He found himself on his back on the bed. Paola handed him a glass of water. 'Have you eaten anything today?'

The water was tepid, with a stagnant taste. He had trouble swallowing. 'Not really.'

Paola nodded an 'of course' nod. 'I better

go down to the *Rosticceria* and get something for supper. Stay still; you need the rest.'

He was exhausted, but lying down didn't help. He was a mass of tight, twitching nerves wrapped around a central emptiness. They had cut out his stomach, cut out, they said, the pain that had lived in him since infancy. But memories could never be cut out. Pain or emptiness? And now they refused to cut into his son, refused to prolong the life, which, limited as it was, was all Francesco had been given. Pain or emptiness? Was there a choice? The phone rang, as he knew it would. He would be firmer with Piero this time. He was tired of being pushed. But, when he picked up the receiver, Adolfo was on the other end.

'We're having an important meeting down here, Marco. We'd certainly appreciate your input.'

'A meeting? What's it about? This is a very bad time for me.' It required such an effort: listening, answering.

'It's concerning the new hotel on the Lido. I thought you'd be anxious to participate on the ground level. Planning to ensure a tasteful, controlled . . .' Adolfo's voice was genial, but the old threat was there, held back but still there.

'At the moment I don't really care . . . Besides, you know and I know that it's all been decided at head office anyway. They've decided what they want. They're just waiting for us to fall in line. Allowing us a bit of pseudo-debate so we have the illusion of "input", as you call it.'

'You go too far. There is no need to be paranoid.'

A faint wail somewhere down the hall. Francesco was awake. 'No need. I said I don't care. Do what you want, what they want, whatever.' The wails were growing louder. 'I have to go.'

'One moment, Marco. This is important. Let me say we realize you are reluctant to participate in the project. If you absolutely refuse — which would not be wise, though there are many others eager to take your place — we still need you at the meeting. There's the question of reassigning you to another project where you wouldn't feel compromised. I suspect the other projects we are to handle will involve a lot more travelling.'

Adolfo did not seem to pause ever for breath. Francesco's cries were getting closer and closer. 'Can't we talk about this Monday?'

'I do understand. It is Saturday afternoon, but Mr. Schmidt from Lucerne will be arriving any moment now. We can't consider only your convenience. It seems imperative that —'

This could go on indefinitely. 'I'm sorry. I'm not feeling well. I'm sure you'll be able to manage fine without me.' And Marco hung up. He let go of a few of the swear words he had been hanging onto. That he had made a mistake, that his refusal would have unfortunate consequences, he had no doubt. But he was tired of the constant juggling for position, the useless meetings, the unstoppable tide of mediocrity, the unstoppable tide of decisions made in Lucerne or New York or even Padova, anywhere but at the place involved, by anyone but the people involved.

Francesco was standing, pants wet and a tear still suspended on his left cheek, in the middle of the hall, chuckling in pleasure at having found his father.

It was soothing to hug him, to hang on tightly to his little squat body, in spite of the wetness and the sharp urine smell. Soothing also to follow the ritual: off with the soggy clothes, on with clean underpants, corduroy slacks, matching suspenders, socks, slippers. Francesco lay unusually still, his face content. Once dressed, he handed his father the bottle of violet essence from the side bureau, a smile, and a high-pitched sigh escaping with the first waves of scent.

Had the familiar already displaced the doctors, the lights, the tubes?

Returning from depositing the clothes in the bathroom, Marco found Francesco merrily tossing the contents of his shelves to the already chaotic floor.

'Why don't we build something?' Marco fished out handfuls of bright plastic blocks from among the myriad of toys. 'Help Daddy, Francesco. Pick up the lego. Help Daddy.'

'Lee go. Lee go.' Francesco kicked open a space in the corner of the area rug. They settled down together. The blocks fit together easily. Francesco immediately began piling them up one on top of the other.

'Let Daddy make you a palace.'

'House,' Francesco said, though he was intent on his own tower.

'Yes, a house.'

It took on an elaborate, symmetrical shape: long galleries, great halls, an impressive staircase. Then, another storey. And always red blocks on one side, blue on the other. Francesco had paused in his own building.

'AAAHHH!' With a whoop, his hand came smashing down, crushing and scattering the newly shaped structure.

'Oh, Francesco,' feeling petty, even as he said it. 'Daddy hadn't finished.' The child was giggling, pulling apart each remaining clump of blocks.

Marco pulled all the bits back and began building again. He tried to involve Francesco, encouraging him to fit the blocks back together. The miniature palace had taken shape again when, with another whoop, Francesco attacked. For a long second, Marco was overwhelmed with the urge to slap that closed, impervious little face. His hand raised itself, started to swing. But the second passed, his fingers met the face in a caress. For below the irritation was a cellular knowledge of the vulnerability of that dumb flesh. Flesh of his flesh. Weakness of his weakness.

Francesco's giggles were going on and on. He was throwing bricks at the walls, the ceiling, out the door, a laughing whirlwind. Through the confusion of anger and affection, Marco caught Francesco's laugh. He let go, letting his laugh match his son's, letting it flow on and on. He began tossing bricks, toys, shoes. A clump of blocks knocked one picture off the wall, a shoe shattered the glass on another. Then, then, he really began to laugh.

XVII

The third time I tried to write of you, I was twenty-two, newly graduated from university and newly involved with Jack. By day I worked as a proofreader, approaching words suspiciously, rigidly. By night I forgot correctness, even clarity, and struggled to find, to shape the meaningful pattern. The Marco that emerged was less dissipated, less charming, and generally less clear than the last version. I was beginning to feel out the links between the bombings, the dislocation, between your father, mother, and brother, and what I perceived you to be now. My heroine, a Canadian girl with a Venetian background, was less innocent, less the victim than my last incarnation, though she was still irritatingly passive, irritatingly 'taken over' at the drop of a hat. I still wanted her destroyed and wanted the destruction to spring from a genetic deficiency, a Venetian inadequacy in the face of the harshness of the new land. But I was starting to realize that downfalls, no matter what the kind, were complex, difficult. So, although you were made to represent the flaw (in full flower, so to speak) you did not carry all the blame. In appropriate and clichéd sixties manner, I threw in drugs. I gave my heroine wondrous acid trips through the history of Venice. (Though my own trips brought not symbol-laden visions but a dull parade of mediocre sights.)

I also gave her (or rather gave myself) lovingly detailed sex scenes. 'Gianni' and 'Serena' were lusty and inventive, coupling in unusual places and positions. Those embarrassing pages make it obvious that, while at fifteen I had been impressed with your sophistication, at twenty-two I was impressed with my own.

'They lie, they lie all the time, so you must ask, doubt, judge for yourself.' It was sound advice and by twenty-two I was grateful for your influence. But an inquiring mind was a hindrance in a school like St. Mary's. If only you could have given me an upturned nose, a really good stereo, or a different nationality.

Like many high schools in the early sixties, status at St. Mary's depended on whether one was accepted into a sorority or not. Pretending superiority, I refused to take the test. Loretta, however, was braver. She had been preparing for a year not just for any sorority but for the most exclusive one, KKG. She had, she thought, all the prerequisites: an approved hairdo, a boyfriend on a school football team, and a pert, pretty face. Her clothes were almost exactly the same as the KKG girls, though she had to rely on the Bay rather than Neiman Marcus, and she had managed to pick up the drawl and turns of phrase favoured by Charlene, the club's president.

It was not enough. She was rejected.

'What did I do wrong?' she demanded of Jody at one of our Saturday afternoon gatherings. 'I did everything right.'

Jody was uncomfortable. She had joined KKG the year before. She had insisted that she didn't particularly want to belong, but her father had laid down the law. 'He says it's important to make the right contacts. Whatever that means.' She insisted I was still her best friend and much more fun than any girl in the sorority. But she enjoyed being one of the inner circle, one of the girls who 'counted'. She alternately had lunch with the one group and with me.

'Jody, answer me. Couldn't you do something?'

'Welll, honey . . .' Jody was starting to do it too. 'It's a bitch. No doubt about that. But you have to face it. I couldn't do anything. You were blackballed, plain and simple.'

We all three took gulps of our favourite brew for such get-togethers — my father's homemade wine diluted with pop. 'Blackballed, why?' Loretta was crying, her voice a little slurred. 'I didn't do nothing wrong. Nothing.'

Jody was patting Loretta on the shoulder. 'I know, honey. It's not you. It's your parents.'

'Her parents?'

'They have an accent.'

'So?' I was getting angry. 'What about Charlene or Georgina or Anna Lee? If you want to talk about accents. What about their parents? They don't talk like Albertans.'

'Don't be obtuse, Bianca. You know what I mean.'

'No, what do you mean?'

'Welll, honey,' you know Ingrid, a class ahead of us? A stunner, right? And her family, they live down the street from us — loaded. And she has all sorts of famous relatives in Europe, concert pianists and all, and she was blackballed on the accent thing. You were aiming too high, Loretta. You have to face reality.'

'KKG reality?' I couldn't help adding. 'Why do you have anything to do with them?'

Jody shrugged her shoulders. 'Lots of reasons. They're not so bad. It's just the rules. Besides you know how much I wanted to make the cheerleading team. I wouldn't have had a chance without their backing. And Daddy represents Charlene's Daddy's oil company.' She was looking sheepish. 'I do disagree with a lot.' She went on to tell us of another classmate, the pretty daughter of a millionaire leader of a political party who was rejected by KKG because her father spoke out against the foreign domination of the oil industry. 'You have to see the context.'

I saw the context, all right. All the seeds of

political theory, the talk of class and colonialism that you had planted in my mind were watered, nurtured.

I finally wanted to come to terms with the country I had been living in. I wanted to make her my country. But she was hidden, obscured. The history, the literature I was taught was English or American. The TV, the movies, the model for life was strictly American. 'In Houston, we . . .' 'Mrs. Kennedy's hat . . .' in the buses and the shops. 'You — Canadians, you are too timid. You don't have the competitive edge.' 'You need us Americans, you need . . .' 'Calgary isn't bad; it's so like Dallas.'

The nuns, faithful companions of Jesus that they were, preached disinterestedness and detachment from the things of this world. They spoke of charity and humility. We were encouraged to bring in our nickels and quarters. Five dollars collected and we could adopt a black child in deepest Africa. Five dollars ensured baptism and rechristening with a name of our choice. So simple, five dollars collected and another soul is saved. Charity was easy, but humility? I remember a tea for two recruiters from an American Catholic university. All the A students and their mothers had been invited. My mother had refused to come. 'What on earth would I say to those women?' And I was both irritated and relieved. I felt exposed without the requisite mother and yet didn't want the deeper exposure of Mamma expounding her opinions with her usual intensity, her usual accent. The other mothers were so nice. They smiled so politely, so fixedly, and they beamed at their adjacent daughters so proudly. Mamma would have been criticizing the sandwiches in English and, more loudly, criticizing the other mothers in Italian. (I was never to forget my graduation from high school. During the final procession in the cathedral, as we filed out, capped and gowned and diplomaed, Mother leaned out from a pew and hissed, 'You look terrible', loudly in English as I passed.)

Unanchored by a mother, I flitted from group to group. But I was sitting alone on a side sofa when I happened to overhear Mother Mary and one of the recruiters talking. Mother Mary was pointing out Anna Lee.'A good student and a good girl. She is so active — in sodality, in student government, a natural leader. She was president of KKC this year too, I think.'

'KKG?' the priest asked in that slightly condescending tone priests use towards nuns.

'A sorority, Kappa Kappa Gamma. All our nicest girls belong. All the girls of quality.'

Bitterness filled my mouth, although she was simply stating a preference that was obvious in the classroom every day.

In those three years after our summer, I had gloried in not being nice. 'If you can't join them, fight them.' I was the class rebel, the one who questioned, challenged, disagreed. 'Why? How can you say . . . If God . . .' You would have approved. The poor teachers took to ignoring my waving hand. I took to skipping classes. They responded with strappings and detentions. They never tried to contact my parents since I pretended they didn't speak English. It was all silly. My rebellion was so petty. I was still easily intimidated. Just last year, I was talking to a woman who attended the school four years after me. Laughing, she told me how she and a friend had stolen the statue of the Madonna out of the front lobby and driven away with it in the back seat of her boyfriend's sports car. I gasped in admiration. I would have never dared. Never. Never.

Yet I thought myself unique. In a blow for liberty, equality, and fraternity, I decided to go to university in Edmonton. The campus was not beautiful but, at least, it did not have the Brasilia-like emptiness of its Calgary counterpart. Mamma, of course, acted as if she were Marie-Antoinette and I was bringing on the Terror. I was flattered, even if deep down I knew I wasn't much of a revolutionary. Those seeds you planted were now in full bloom. I went to meetings — endless meetings. I helped organize demonstrations. I joined a collective. We studied so seriously. Not only your Marx and Lenin, but Fanon, Guevera, Marcuse, Mao. I became a spokesman, a speaker to less enlightened groups. We were fueled by our anti-Americanism. My special friend at the time (the one who had my picture blown up) loved to fantasize the Americans invading and the two of us guerillas. Lightheadedly, we planned strategies as we drove around in his red battered Volkswagen.

In those university years, I had to give up my visits to Venice for summer jobs and short visits to Vancouver and Montreal. The parental wallet was firmly closed, but I knew from your letters and my earlier visits that my 'political' life, my days passed with my 'gang', *in gruppo*, after accounting for cultural differences, were similar to your days. After our summer you had made a decision; you had found a type of direction. You stopped painting, you returned to high school, went on to university. But your new resolve did not pull you off what for the city was the ancient way, the path of pleasure, the enjoyment that lay in the expanses of unfettered time. There was always time to sleep until noon, time to wander from bar to bar, club to club, in search of 'good times', time to lie abed with a new woman and learn each curve, test each response. Time — even for me.

Yet when I finally did come for a week, after a couple of months at a summer school in Rome, I found you bound, tied. You had left the sun-filled path. The brightness of the days eventually only emphasized the emptiness. The centre of each pleasure harboured the seed of anxiety; the search for enjoyment had become desperate, almost frenzied. So, you had made a further decision. You were engaged, and it was an engagement that seemed to demand your dancing in attendance. Now you had not time for even a coffee with me. 'I promised Paola.' 'Sorry, I can't.' 'Paola's expecting me.'

I wanted to ask of Elena, but you gave me no chance. It was your mother who told me she had gotten married a few months before. I did catch you alone in the kitchen late one night, fixing yourself some camomile.

'It seems so sudden.'

'Sudden.' You smiled. 'Not at all. I'm more than old enough.'

'I thought everyone in Italy had enormously long engagements.'

'Everyone, not I. It's right for me now. Finally one must put away the childish life of the senses. If one stays too long one becomes ridiculous.'

I asked, 'Are you in love with Paola?'

You gestured towards your cup. 'I told you years ago that I couldn't remain a tour guide, that I needed a more serious focus. If one cannot paint, one can at least design. One must plunge into adult life. One must take one's place.'

'But are you in love with her? *Sei inammorato di lei?*'

You blinked as if surprised. 'Naturally — *Le voglio bene.*' (I have much affection for her.)

Even then you couldn't say you were in love with her.

'*Le vuoi bene?*' I was determined to push my point, but you deflected it.

'Still the sentimentalist, Bianca? Two meet, their eyes fuse, a lightning bolt flashes out of the sky. They are transformed. *Ah, Bambinona.* You'll learn.' You pinched my cheek. I slapped at your hand.

Paola did send me an invitation to tea — a great honour, according to your mother and sister who were yet to be invited. And, sitting on a blue velvet armchair in her living room across from the two of you, I could see, if not the idea of the marriage, at least the seed of the concept, the original attraction. Paola was so solid, so immovably certain. There would be no floating with her. She was the lady at home with frescoes and persian rugs to mark her boundaries. Her manicured fingers on the white china pot. 'Lemon or rum? With this dreadful rain today I thought . . . You are sure no rum? It does one good.'

Beside her you were pale and gaunt, all bones and nerves. The bourgeois woman, a man said to me once, is the ultimate love object. Charlene, Anna Lee, Paola. The rest of us, even Elena, can never offer the security, the sureness of self, the possibility of balance.

'Another biscuit? No? What were we saying? Ah yes, I was asking if this BA of yours was equivalent to the *magistrale* degree here.' Her condescension was a wrought iron barrier keeping me firmly removed from your life together.

That barrier remained until the last time I saw the two of you. Whether my better status — I was no longer just a student; I was travelling with a lover — or whether the burden of Francesco had removed it, I don't know. Paola was different. Her solidity was now edged with flutter. Her hands shook when she handed me an aperitif, and during dinner she flitted back and forth from dining room to kitchen, not just to transfer dishes but to check on Francesco who was eating there with her mother. When she was sitting at the table with us, she was voluble, wandering, with no reference to what we were talking about, in, out, and around topics: fashions, universities, your mother, strikes, the capping of the artesian wells, doctors.

You made no move to help her. You sat comfortably, expecting the service. You had trained Paola almost as well as your mother. 'We need more bread . . . another bottle of mineral water.'

I interrupted Paola, who was asking about the price of mink coats in Canada and passing the salad.

'One difference between here and there is the men. In Canada, among educated people particularly,' I was exaggerating, lying almost, 'antiquated roles are passing away. There is a true movement towards equality. The men are secure enough in their maleness to cook, to look after the babies and not feel diminished but rather enriched.'

Both of you jumped in. Paola insisting on the petty, the childish, the tyrannical nature of Italian men; you insisting that it was the nature of Italian women that could properly be described as such. 'Equality is one thing — here women rule. Italy is a matriarchy.' The tendency of both of you, evident since the beginning of the visit to try to prove the other wrong escalated into all-out hostilities.

'Don't be so stupid.'

'I wouldn't use the word stupid. If anyone . . .'

Neither of you would give in on even the most negligible point. Each of your statements was clung to as infallible. I was embarrassed and, though I could tell that you were both enjoying it, I was angry with you. You were ever so slightly the more aggressive, the more extreme. I saw you reduce yourself to a sneer.

You were both going to walk me to the *vaporetto*, but when we were about to leave, Francesco and Paola's mother happened to emerge from the kitchen. Seeing both you and Paola about to go out, he set up a howl, loud and anguished. Paola immediately dropped to her knees and put her arms around him. She spoke softly and slowly. 'Mommy and Daddy are going out for a very little while. We will be back immediately. In no time at all.' Francesco kept howling. Paola turned to us. 'Maybe you'd better go without me.'

'Paola.' Your voice was mild, inquiring, 'the doctor said we mustn't give in on everything. We must be firm. He must learn . . .'

Paola had turned back to Francesco, 'Learn? Please go. It'll be faster.'

Outside, 'You see, you see what my life is, Bianca?'

'I see.'

'It doesn't go with Paola and me. It doesn't work.'

How could I reply? You shouldn't have said it to me. You owed her that. You wanted to say more, but I didn't want to hear.

'You're wise not to marry.'

It was the last time I saw you. When you kissed me goodbye at the *vaporetto*, you stared into my eyes. You wanted something. *'Sempre semplice.'* Always simple. 'Little cousin.'

Always simple, an accusation and a dismissal. I have been accused and dismissed for being the opposite: subtle and obscure. 'After I wrote that third novel, I took it to a summer writing school in Saskatchewan. The class, a reasonably small one, consisted of the usual mixture of the serious and the frivolous, the talented and the ambitious. They read my manuscript, then shook their heads, and closed ranks against me. It was like being in elementary school again. 'Subtle, obscure, needlessly complex,' they all agreed, even the very subtle Canadian

Writer. The worst transgression of all was my writing of Italy. 'Why?' they asked. 'Why not write of here? You can never do it well. Not like an Italian would. Give it up.' And what they didn't say, but was heard. 'Be like us.' They wrote of the land, of growing up on farms, of battling the elements, of the strain of moving to the city. They felt themselves morally superior in their simplicity and clarity, superior in their true communion with the land. How could I explain that rural Western Canada was as alien to me as Venice to them? How could I tell them beyond 'I know Venice?' Likewise, when the pretty blonde with the head of curls, working on a book that enumerated the trials and tribulations of a Saskatoon housewife, challenged me with, 'What about female conciousness? You should be giving voice to that. Who cares about this man?' How could I answer? I had no valid reasons. I wrote of Venice. I wrote of you, and I still do, not from choice but need. We must each of us stare into the lion's mouth.

XVIII

The edge of the horizon: heavy grey sky pressing down, resistant grey sea answering with even more agitated waves, answering with white foam, the only demarcation of limit. But just beyond the edge, a new fulcrum of sea and sky: the waves had thrown up a floating city chipped from petrified salt crystals, a city where grey was divided into the extremities of stone and water, light and dark.

The rush of steam, vapour made coffee, in the espresso pot on the stove, brought Marco back. Again he found himself, this time at the kitchen table. The rich, familiar scent of coffee filling the room, a sweet, acidic taste on his tongue. Arranged on a white plate before him was a circle of orange sections; two pieces were missing. One piece, smooth and damp, was poised between the thumb and forefinger of his right hand, which was also lying on the table, also distinct-edged, yet so far, far away.

Paola, her chin high, was entering the kitchen with Francesco. Her large glittering eyes seemed about to jump out of her head. She suspected, oh yes, she suspected. She'd been in the boy's room, where else? He had one of those silly embroidered bibs around his neck.

Marco lifted his hand to his mouth and bit into the fruit. Such fleshy sweetness: the essence of exotic flowers blooming under a hot sun. And he would have asked the name of this unfamiliar tropical fruit, but Paola spoke first.

'What were you thinking of? I had to change Francesco's sweater. Didn't you notice how much he was dribbling? You know he should wear a bib.'

'No. I didn't notice.' Staring down at the fruit sections on the plate. How could he have forgotten it was an orange? Breaking open a section, exposing the scarlet-filamented orange pulp. A blood orange, that was all. Yet the taste, biting down, the spray on the roof of his mouth — so strange, so unlike anything he had known.

Paola had crossed to the stove and was turning off the burner beneath the pot. 'It's all up to me, isn't it?' Those deep lines were visible again even in the muted afternoon light. 'All up to me.'

Francesco gaped at them, a translucent thread of saliva hanging to his feet. 'I'll take him down to the den. You get the cups.'

'We need to talk.'

'I'm coming back.'

Marco settled Francesco on the sofa, then flicked through the multi-channels. Brief glimpses of a nostalgia comedy show, a naked woman fully turned to the camera, a political panel debate, Bob Dylan singing in Arab head-dress and, finally, Tom and Jerry cartoons. He could have so easily gone on, round and round, sixteen channels, click, click, click. Marco handed the channel changer to his son who was already totally taken up with the action and the colour on the screen.

Back in the kitchen, Paola was sitting, staring into her coffee. Her cheeks and neck were flushed deep red.

'So what are these momentous decisions you've made?' Not bad. An effort, this trying to stay focused, trying to avoid being caught up by an object, a colour, a ray of light.

Her skin seemed to take on an even deeper shade of redness. 'Listen, I've finally understood. If we are going to have another chance, we must have another child.' She must have rehearsed it, even to the expression, chin in the air, eyes level.

'Another chance. Too much chance.' She was his wife. They had slept side by side for ten years, slept, eaten, been. She was his wife, as much an unconscious part of himself as his nails or hair and, in essence, as unknown, as mysterious. She was part of him and yet not part, for across the table she seemed utterly strange, utterly alien to his flesh.

'When we were in Padova a month ago, do you remember, I went to see Dr. Sabatini, the gynaecologist. I didn't tell you but he tested me. Took a genetic smear.'

'It must have been when Francesco and I went to look at the Giotto frescoes. Yes?'

'Anyway, the results have come back. There's no reason why I couldn't have a normal child. Of course, you'd have to be tested too before we went ahead.'

She had made her mind up a long time ago, before the first test probably. He both would have liked her to know and feared her knowing his irrational conviction that only abnormalities, defects could spring from his flesh. Not that it would show in a test. No, the flaw was of the spirit. Emptiness made flesh. 'You're getting sillier every day,' she would say. 'I've never heard anything more ridiculous' and maybe he'd be able to believe her.

'What if we check out fine and we still . . . we could still conceive . . .' The coffee was hot, sweet, satisfying.

Paola set down her cup in the saucer with an impatient click. 'But things have changed. They've developed these tests. When the foetus is about fifteen weeks old. First they perform an ultrasound scan. This enables them to see the size of the foetus and how it's lying. Then they introduce a needle through the womb into the amniotic fluid. They remove a few cc's of the fluid, and since it contains discarded foetal cells, they can analyse the foetus's genetic makeup as well as test for a broad range of diseases. So you can know . . . and if it's bad, something can be done. One doesn't have to be at the mercy of . . .'

Her colour was still high, but now it was lit with the brightness of hope rather than nerves. 'It doesn't have to be chance. Medical science has achieved wonders these last few years. It's made the impossible possible. It's quite miraculous.'

Miraculous: that they should understand the secret laws by which the universe was ordered to such an extent that they could see the foetus in the womb, that they could examine the microscopically small discarded cell of an unborn child and be able to classify, to judge. Miraculous yet contradictory: because the knowledge was based on a presumption of a hidden but rational order; yet, behind the act, behind the classification was the assumption of the lack of order, the lack of laws, the absence of Providence; an assumption that variants were not to be valued simply as God's chosen creatures. ('Are not two sparrows sold for a farthing and one of them shall not fall in the grass without your father knowing. The very hairs of your head are all numbered.') An assumption that variants should be seen as worthless, chaotic matter.

'Aren't you going to say anything?' Paola was staring at him. How could he tell her that in order to conceive new life he would need to believe in Providence and purpose and,

235

then, there would be no question of tests, only acceptance. His belief had been cut out of him so long ago that normally he felt no loss, but in the last few days the old wound had begun to ache again. He wished for the support it would have given, the conviction that was twisted deep down in his guts, the conviction of the sanctity of life.

'And Francesco? Doesn't he take all we have? We would end up either depriving the new child or him.'

'All you have perhaps,' she retorted quickly, then, just as quickly, shook her head. 'No. I'm sorry. I mean, I don't agree. It doesn't work like that. You'll see.'

Fleetingly, he considered bringing out the ring. It would be appropriate — the early present. And gentleness and pliancy might just be bought by diamond and sapphire. But he no longer had the energy for the necessary accompanying gestures and words. Tomorrow.

'We don't have to decide right now, do we? Later, when I'm feeling better, when my mind is clearer.'

Paola's chin was still up, determined. 'I've already decided. I told you.'

She knew he was not quite himself, that he was weakened, and she was going to take advantage of it. He must hold fast. He must. 'Just a few minutes ago you were distraught over Francesco, and all that won't go away with another child. It will only be more complicated. And what about our problems? Do you think a baby will solve those?'

'Will not having one solve them? I doubt it. Can't you see it could give us the balance we need.'

The telephone's summoning bell, almost welcome, if only he didn't fear who could be on the other end. 'If it's for me,' he told Paola who was already up and at the door of the den, 'I'm not available. Adolfo's insisting on my going in to work.'

Francesco was lying sideways across the padded arm of the sofa, head down, rocking on his belly, all the battered leather within his reach decorated with long saliva streaks. On the unwatched TV, Ironarm (Popeye) and Brutus were taking turns hitting each other on the head with giant mallets. Marco rescued the channel changer from the floor, bestowing a short caress on his son's back both on the way down and on the way back up. After the third channel switch (past a spaghetti western and the Incredible Hulk), he paused. A glamorous blonde announcer was in the middle of a news flash. The chief prosecutor for the Veneto, who had been instrumental in obtaining severe penalties for several known Padova terrorists, had been assassinated.

Francesco, who had somehow slid to the floor, was pulling on his pant leg, but Marco stood motionless. The beautiful announcer, rounded syllables and all, had been replaced by a folk-rock star seemingly trying to swallow a microphone, but still he couldn't move.

Paola entered, 'I've been calling you. Phone.'

'I can't talk now.'

'Listen, it's your Aunt Elsa. You tell her you can't talk. I've given her the news from Padova, so it's not that. She didn't seem particularly interested, though, I must say. And she's very insistent.'

'I . . . '

'Marco . . . for the love of God.'

Elsa began by expressing the conventional regrets. But Paola was right. Underneath the politeness was an edginess and what was more unusual, a lack of attention to Marco's replies.

'Zia, what's happened?'

'A disaster, Marco, a disaster. And I need your advice. I don't know what to do. It's Barbara.'

'Barbara?'

'There was an assassination. Those pigs. She was out buying some socks, said she had to have them, you know what they're like, she and Patrizia. By Via Frecceria, near the *Piazza*.'

'In Venice? I didn't think . . . She saw it happen?' Little, grey-eyed Barbara.

'No. No. Not quite. But she was so close. She heard the shots. Then, she saw the body lying on the steps.' It would stay with her. Hover in her mind as long as she lived. Unless, of course, she saw worse and the new horrors burned out the old. 'It's too dreadful. I don't know how she got home, but she's in pieces, simply pieces. I can't calm her. She keeps talking about the blood and the way the body was turned. Should I try to get Tarquinio, that's what I want to know? He and Lea have enough on their hands at the hospital and Lea being in a state as it is. You know her nerves . . . '

'Call Tarquinio. He'd want you to. Oh, and the doctor. He can prescribe something.'

'Yes. Yes, I didn't think of that. I knew you'd know the right thing to do . . . You couldn't . . . no? Oh, Marco, Marco, the days we're living through. There's no order. There's no respect. That's why God must send us another war that will teach people. They must pay for the way they live. The rottenness.'

Marco was speechless although he had heard variations on the theme from Elsa before; variations always delivered in the same tone — one degree from hysteria. Finally mastering his rage, he managed: 'Listen to what you're saying. Think. You can't mean it.'

'Another war. I've lived through two. I know what I'm saying. And I know what people deserve.'

But it's not the people and us; we're also the people, Marco wanted to cry out, but there were important details to establish. It could be a coincidence. He must stay clear. 'When exactly did it happen?'

'She said she was going shopping. You

never know, of course, but let that pass. Had to have new tights. She never got there.'

'What time?'

'Well, it must have been around four. It was just a little while ago.'

Four. If the water goes down . . . There was no more room for evasion, no more room for doubt and, as suddenly, the leap was made. Marco knew, he felt, he was the victim.

A soft-bodied young man in an old black coat, not looming, no, but there, with the air of a fixture, leaning against one of the ancient, faceless statues in the corner of the small square. I can see him staring at me from underneath his flat cap. Staring, recognizing, a smile crumbling his flat face, wrinkling his thin moustache. He is a good twenty feet away, but I know irretrievably that our locked gazes are portentous, that he has recognized me in a way I have never been recognized before. I turn to my colleague. There is still much not said, in spite of the long meeting we've endured. 'Let's go this way,' he says. 'The Piazza's impossible today. They're having a demonstration against nuclear energy.' His hand directing by pressure on my elbow. Strange he cannot hear the beating of my heart. Blood pounding. Even the other people in the square seem to be moving to the rhythm. Only the man in the black coat, only he is still rhythmless, staring.

How shabby the buildings look in the afternoon light, tacky stage sets. I don't feel the hero. My breath quickens, rasps. I must move. But my foot slips, stone and water. Sprawling exposed, winded, on the bottom steps, so smooth and damp beneath me . . . Careless. Pina was right. (I should have.) Cared more. He's pointing a short squat gun. Never thought they'd choose me, never thought they'd try here, inviolate Venice. Careless. My mouth opens. My heartbeats deafen me. A bright flare at the end of the gun. Caught on a stone tooth. Pinned to hardness. Enough pain, more than enough. The barrier's gone. Masks gone. Not everyone sees. Another flare lighting up the grey waiting sea.

Sunset — New Day

XIX

The façades of the palaces along the Grande Canale seemed ablaze in pink, fleshy light, the last rays of the sun coaxing out the salmon-coloured veins of the Verona stone. Marco stood alone on the prow of the *vaporetto*, away from those going only one or two stops, impatiently sandwiched into the centre of the others, going farther, who sat comfortable in the heated, covered section. Many of the palaces were showing signs of decrepitude, signs that had been rare, Marco remembered, even ten or fifteen years ago. Pollution from Mestre had loosened mosaics, eaten into the thin veneer of marble, exposing the brick base. Still, in the sunset light one could ignore the gaps in the illusion. The mask seemed intact.

And Marco himself, as he stood with his legs ever adjusting to the sway of the *vaporetto*, felt curiously intact — all his contradictions pulled into a unified whole by the intensity of his outrage. How dare they? He said it so often to himself it became a chant. How dare they involve him in such an abhorrent thing. How dare they use him as if he were a mere instrument? He would not stand for it.

He would no longer acquiesce from cowardice and uncertainty. No. Enough.

A funeral barge laden with enormous pink and red carnation crosses was approaching from the opposite direction, forcing a channel through the jam of water taxis and vegetable-laden market boats by sheer moral superiority. As it drew up level with the *vaporetto*, however, a gondola ferry a few yards ahead caused a momentary pause. The reclining gold lion facing Marco (there was one, as was traditional, on each side) seemed to stare up balefully at him with his empty, metal eyes. I know you. 'I know who you are,' Elena had said, 'progressive . . . correct . . .' And they had known who he was and what he thought and stood for, and still they had made him the messenger of death. How skillfully they had woven the web that linked him to the black barge. Skillfully. Expertly.

Where were they now? In some anonymous room, the blankness of white walls cut only by the red, spray-painted slogans. Elena, naked, face down on the unmade bed, Piero standing beside, cock up, but still detached, using more than his stubby fingers, using the jargon, the plotting, the idea of destruction, the idea of the gun in the hand and the blood on the stone step to make her swampish with desire.

He had to free himself of that web. He had to rip those sticky bonds or be caught forever — impotent and voyeuristic.

Kill or be killed, Piero had said, the easiest thing in the world.

He would denounce them and face the consequences. They thought they were safe with him. 'How could we act if it wasn't for thousands of smaller, supporting actions?' Piero had asked, but this act called for denunciation by any man of conscience. Not that he fooled himself about the type of justice the judicial system could mete out. Or even that he saw them guilty of executing an innocent man, a good man. The brigades would have cause. They were not fascists indiscriminately bombing banks or train stations.

Kill or be killed, the easiest thing in the world. Of course it was easy, too easy. One second a man, the next . . . Betrayers. Traitors. Venice had been immune from the easy killings that infected the rest of Italy as she had been immune from assassinations, uprisings, conquerors, for hundreds of years. Now the germ was introduced. No wonder Dante reserved the lowest circle of hell for traitors. Canto XXXIII. Elena and Piero frozen to their tears in iced canals. He would gladly walk on their heads. He could feel the curliness of Elena's hair beneath his feet, hear her groans in his ears. Condemned to eternal ice, to eternal humiliation. Careful. He must not lose himself again. Control. Still, they deserved to have the full wrath of the state called down upon them. The hooded inquisitors would have their way.

The *vaporetto* stop. He leapt off just as the metal rails were closing, almost knocking over a woman with a child in a stroller in his haste. If only he could avoid his own exposure, for it was not only that he would be exposed in his inadequacy, in his faithlessness, to Paola and his family, but he and his whole family would be exposed to the world. Like that landlady of the two female brigadists in Rome. Her entire life had been paraded through the gossip magazines. Dignity in such situations was difficult. One fell into the most extreme of stances: indignant citizen, duped friend. One could only try to avoid descending to the most common trick — whining for pity. 'I'm a simple, good man, wanting all that we simple good men want, little knowing . . .'

If he could keep his part hidden. A secret denunciation. Black letters on parchment paper, look to such and such, enemies of the Republic. Elena wouldn't be difficult to trace. Whatever else she had become, she was still the faithful Italian daughter. There would be at least a phone call, if not a visit to her mother every week. And under the right type of questioning, under the right type of pressure . . . He could see her face: her beauty no longer just greyed, but cracked, the features disassociated, crumbling. She would break and deliver up her revered comrade.

Before him, a long-haired young boy pushing an enormous basket wheelbarrow. Marco turned sideways and pressed himself to the brick wall, letting the contraption past. The exhilaration he felt at imagining Elena shattered was hard and solid like the ridge of brick pushing into his back. But attacking that hardness, like acid rain, was anguish.

Could the old Elena, his Elena, the present self shed, emerge from such a rupture? Or was she not simply locked away but gone? Strange that after all that had happened he could still long for her. Strange that with the pleasure at the thought of her pain came his, as if his flesh cried out at his thoughts.

One Sunday afternoon. He must have been in his mid teens. His family had been having dinner with hers and was still all around the table. Elena was standing, passing out dessert plates, bending over to reach the centre of the table to deposit the platter of pastries. Her dress was sleeveless and as blue as her eyes, her golden hair tied at the nape of her neck. She was so artlessly clear, so artlessly beautiful. He was blinded to anything else in the room, though his mind, slightly removed from the swell of feelings within him, calmly evaluated. So this is what love is — what I feel just at the sight of her. (Let it be my measuring stick.) Then, his father, as if acting upon Marco's sensations, grabbed Elena's bare arm as she was straightening. 'Look at this.' He pinched the tight, tanned skin. His face was reddened from the copious wine, his mouth slack. No, that leering was a twist, a perversion of Marco's desires. 'Young flesh. That's what a man needs, not these baggy bitches. A taste of this.' He bent as if to bite. His mother and Elena's mother were laughing uneasily; they were determined, it seemed, to keep the situation unimportant. On Elena's transparent face amusement and revulsion warred for control.

'Papa!' Marco was on his feet, ready to leap across the table. But his father had already let go, his thick hands wrapped back around his glass of wine.

His father laughed. 'Regard this young cock, feathers ruffled, strutting away.' Marco was irresolute, torn between following Elena's graceful back out of the room or facing down his father. A long time ago. Marco couldn't remember how it turned out. He probably had argued until his father had pulled out his usual insult; how Marco still had shit on his nightshirt. That remark always reduced Marco to such sheer, dumb rage that his mother had to step in.

A long time ago. But his memory of the openness, the expressiveness of Elena's face, *that* foolishly remained alive and immediate. What had made her turn to masks, to deceits? Now she used her whole body to deceive.

The *calle* opened into Campo Manin, crowded, as it always was at the end of the day, with gangs of young people. Talk, laughter, smoke, flirtation: the endless rituals. Many had attended the demonstration. He heard fragments, comments on the speakers, the behaviour of other parts of the crowd, as he wound his way through the animated clusters. Still, now the atmosphere was relaxed. They were there to see and be seen and to plan the evening ahead. He had been one of them once. He had been one of them until Paola.

He had loved her and, yes, part of that had involved loving her apartment, her parents, such a polite contrast to his own, her air of breeding, her knowledge of the correct act, the correct word at the correct time. She was to have been his centre, his balance. But the very qualities he had hungered for turned sour in the eating. And instead of balancing, she had weighed him down, ground him into the human mire.

Another chance, she had said, another chance. They were beyond chances, beginnings. Beyond, yet still irretrievably bonded, Francesco's birth an indestructible cement.

The *mercerie,* one glittering shop window after another, the paths clogged by the slow-moving, window-shopping families, their different voices combining into a high-pitched cheerful hum. Only one window out of the many drew Marco, causing a short halt in his journey. It featured a display of Venetian artisanry: a milky-white glass vase, an ornate silver picture frame, several beautifully bound books, a bolt of Fortuny material and, balanced on sticks so they seemed to overlook the other objects, a variety of leather masks. Staring at one in particular, a black half-mask with a delicate lace border, intimation of the previous night's dream floated up into his consciousness. The mouth. The Ferris wheel.

In startling suddenness, his stomach, so unusually sensationless in the last few hours, was gripped in pain, forcing him to double over, one arm across his middle, one out to the shop window. It ebbed slowly, allowing Marco gradually to straighten himself. Control, careful. The street was jammed with curious eyes. One last look at the window before pushing himself on. The artisans of Venice. The continuation of one thousand years of shaping by the human hand. The artisans of Venice, doomed like their city, in a world of Adolfo's. The human hand. And that which is formed by the will? the dream? the flesh?

Paola had complicated strategies for the remaking of Francesco. A special education teacher for several hours in the morning, systems of behaviour modification practised by the whole family, a special diet with megavitamins and, most essentially, the right heart surgeon in Texas or Canada, or wherever he might be. As if she thought it actually possible to remake the boy.

Such frailty of mind and body; the confusion, the stunted words, the shortness of breath, the blueness of hue at every exertion.

Francesco clinging to his leg, his puffy slanted eyes staring up at him, not saying, never being able to say, but Marco still heard the words, echoes of Dante. 'Father, you do not help me.' It was he — not Elena and Piero — who was confined, like Ugolino to the last circle of hell. And like Ugolino, his damnation rested on the thought of his child's need. 'Father, you dressed me in this flesh, undress me now.' He was responsible for what Francesco was, and it was his responsibility to free him from the maze of limitations.

It would be so easy — a pillow, a few seconds. Who would suspect? Hadn't they warned over and over that it could happen from one moment to the next. A pillow. No, better, a doubling of his heart medicine. Easier and so undetectable. Then all the waiting would be over. Release for both of them. Francesco freed, returned to the spirit. 'Undress me now.'

No. Running now through the patches of light and dark, past the murmuring crowd. No, it was not his thought but an alien idea that forced itself in during a moment of weakness. It was the one thing he had never wanted. Always life, never death. Never.

But then, he heard the flinty roar of the lion. Layers beneath layers, truths beneath truths. Coward, the lion roared, self-deceiver. Death is not only without but within. Victimizer and victim. And again Marco's mind leapt.

My eye is acute. I see immediately the best place. A dark, shaded corner of the square, beside two faceless old statues that can serve as leaning posts or believable objects of observation, if the need to dissemble arises. The square is almost empty; no cops, uniformed or not. Only I stand waiting. My view of the steps is clear, the angle good. My metal bolt lies prepared, beautifully heavy and solid in my left pocket. My hands are trembling. I will steady them when the moment comes. I will not fail. The transformation will occur. My flesh will be fused into steel, tool of future generations. The doors open. It is not him. I memorized the pictures almost too well. I began to sense the man behind the surface grain. This time. Yes. The man on the left. English tweed suit, cashmere coat on the shoulders, sleek groomed head. He signals what he is. The anger, clean and pure, rising, pooling the hot salty saliva in my mouth. His head turns, our eyes meet across the stony expanse. He knows. The sudden birth of terror. My fingers, steady and strong now, draw out the weapon. And he falls, weak in the face of wrath. Spread out, he is an easy target for my practised hand. My body poised, subservient to the finger on the trigger. One. Perfect. Two. The blood visible now. My blood exultant. The joyous clarity of action.

The exaltation was in Marco's blood, the anger, the ability to destroy, not just a stranger on some stone stairs but his own flesh. No wonder he could not evade the young man's smell, a faint trace of it clung still. It was his smell too. 'Know your own stink.' He had thought that, by his standing back, he could see the hidden corners of the mind. Perhaps those of others, but he had never dared gaze into his own.

Now was the time to stare into the mouth of the lion. And, of course, it was for this purpose, without realizing it, that he had begun this walk through the city. His feet had been carrying him not to the authorities but to the place where he had to go. A few more steps and he was out from the *Calle delle Razze* and on the broad expanse of the *Riva degli Schiavoni*. The sun was in the final stages of setting behind the line of the Lido. The lagoon was a smooth crimson carpet. The palaces, now on his right, were at their most graceful and dignified. The air was filled with music, not Vivaldi, Gabrieli, Albinoni, or even Mahler, but with the tinselly tunes of the fair. Like apparitions, the rides perched on the *Riva*, their bright coloured lights eclipsed by the last traces of the sunset.

Although *carnevale* was just beginning, many in the crowd that promenaded up and down before the rides, or waited eagerly in line for their two minutes of delicious fear, were in costumes. A witch and a skeleton were settling into the bottom chair of the Ferris wheel.

Two bunnies arm in arm pushed past him, gig-
gling. And when Marco finally stopped walk-
ing, and planted himself in preparation before
the parachute drop, he was nearly knocked
over by a thuggish-looking young man in a
draped sheet with a crown of leaves on his
head. Around his neck, he wore a handwritten
sign — VIRGILIO. 'Scuse me.' Virgil's arm
flailed around Marco's neck in his attempt to
straighten himself. His breath on Marco's face
was Scotch heavy. 'These damn skirts.' Marco
hurriedly shoved Virgil back to an upright posi-
tion. 'OK, OK, OK,' but once he was gone,
weaving his way towards the merry-go-round,
Marco was almost sorry. Any distraction was
preferable to standing alone in this merry-
making crowd, waiting. It was coming, the
memory, making its way up closer and closer.
His stomach, his whole body was trying to
tense against it. 'I can't,' his mind said, 'I can't
go through it all again. I can't look again and
still be.' His breath was agitated, his head spin-
ning, but something held firm.

*Mother holding his hand, pulling him faster
than his short legs can manage. Shaking,
partly from the cold. Because of their haste,
they are coatless. 'Hurry.' Mother keeps say-
ing. 'Hurry. Dear God.' Planes. Their roar ever
closer above. Bangs, ever louder, behind.
'Bombs, bombs, when will it finish?' Mother
says. 'Hurry. We're almost out . . . the*

farm . . .' Then, in front, a bright orange ex-
plosion. Mother on her knees, arms around
him, tears wetting his shoulder. But they walk
again, run. Around the corner the rides still
twirling, but off, the music off, the twirling
off. What? Mother's hands down over his eyes.
Darkness, only the speeded up, hysterical
music far off yells like howling dogs. A louder
bang. The ground shaking under their feet. A
scream. Mother's. He sees the parachute ride
turning at a crooked angle, the people in the
seats disjointed, floppy. Her hands again. One
to cover his eyes, one to guide him. 'Mamma,
I'll fall' — so she moves the fingers back until
they rest on the side of his head like blinkers.
An enormous bang, the orange glow lighting
up the death rides. The empty merry-go-round
spinning ever faster, the Ferris wheel seats tip-
ping out bodies. Wetness on his face. A dark
rain. Wiping away. Blood on his hand. Mother
crouched whimpering on the ground. Another.
Pieces of bodies hanging in the trees above. A
raw arm. Two legs. Exposed innards. The
blood dripping on his face and hands.

Marco was shaking, his body twitching as
if conducting an electric current. That memory,
though unremembered, the centre of every-
thing he was to become. Those body parts fes-
tooning the trees. Man below the masks, below
the skin, undifferentiated flesh. One intestine
like another intestine, one heart like another
heart. Anonymous, cheap. To kill or be killed,

the easiest thing in the world. Note well the lion's roar.

Quick. Move. No time to savour what I and my gun can do. No time to stand in the full flower of my strength. Chin in the air, foot on the body: hero at the barricades, transformed utterly. My foot is light. I float around the closest corner, over the bridge, down the calle, *through the arcade. I grow heavier as the danger ebbs. The* Piazza *is packed with the demonstrators. The usual bourgeois types: oozing their concern for the 'environment', designer-checked work shirts, perfectly cut corduroys. Still, to most eyes I blend in. Tuck my cap in my pocket. The gun. I didn't think what to do with it. A canal? No. Not out of the maze yet. Another need could arise. The hue must be up, but I make my way to the* vaporetto *with no hassle. Piazzale Roma, the train station, even the Lido ferry will be watched. Yet they will not find me — a phantom beyond their reach. Moored on the* zattere, *my boat a common enough looking fishing boat. Oars. They won't guess escape by sea. Venice's old protectoress. Or realize that I know each sand bar, each shoal in the lagoon. Who will check the backwaters of Chioggia? One more fishing boat arrives with the dawn. To strike in the heart of Venice and escape. The impossible accomplished. Only the cries of the seagulls on this limitless flat expanse. Pale orange sky and sea. Oars retracted, I raise my sail. It is painted in the old Chioggian manner. A giant eye and a star, all contained in a triangle. Ancient mumbo jumbo. Slowly, gently, the sail catches the breeze and, without limits, I am skimming away.*

Night. Marco finds himself in darkness on the top of the Paglia Bridge, staring out at the black lagoon and the sparse lights of the winter Lido. He knows there can be no escape once the sharp-toothed lion has bitten. He is caught, he must finish his role, he must make his denunciation. *Pax tibi Marce aevangeli stameus.* Peace only through the bringing of the truth to life. Peace only through bearing witness to that truth. Peace, as long as the winged lion still held the book open.

Walking slowly past the south side of the ducal palace, past the ladies and their *ciscebei* on their evening stroll, past the courtesans smiling arm in arm, past the Levantine merchants, the Arabic beggars, the jugglers, the booths. Turning into the Piazzetta, past the covey of deserted gondolas tied to the striped moorings, past the Marciana library, past the two columns where sometimes gallows were raised, one column bearing St. Theodore and his crocodile, the other his own winged lion, past the lacy, harmonious palace arches, past the *campanile* where Galileo first looked through a telescope, where prisoners were sometimes kept in cages to suffer the effects of the elements. Each stone in this city containing story over story, layer over layer of human history.

Who could choose the essential one? The true one?

Turning to *Porta della Carta*, past the Moors, claimed to be Saracens but actually Roman tetrachs, past the expanse of mosaicked marble on the church's side with its central panel of sea green. Into the tunnel, out across the inner courtyard, up the Staircase of the Giants, along the *loggia*. Odd how empty, how silent the palace was. It waited for him and the truth he had to tell. *La bocca di leone*, the mouth of the lion was difficult to find in the dim light, made as it was out of the same stone as the rest of the wall. *Bocca di leone*, terror of the city, receptacle of denunciation, tool of the hooded inquisitors, purveyor of savage, unquestionable justice. The mouth of the lion, finally, in front of him. *DENOTIE SECRETE.* Carefully pulling out pen and paper. *Pax tibi Marce.* Writing large the letters of the killer's name. MARCO BOLCATO, GUILTY. Pushing the sheet in the mouth already crammed with other paper. Guilty. *Bocca di leone*, the stretched mouth of a man in agony without end.

Epilogue

XX

Venice, stone and water, Venice, bride of the sea, bride of my dreams; she is the recurring motif that I cannot escape and I cannot capture. I have dreamt each method of approach. By plane, the flat land gives way to delta, the low plain etched by a myriad of rivers and tributaries into an abstract print. The lagoon is marked by shoals, by mud islands. And as we dip, as we drop lower and lower, the city lies below me: a red-roofed tight maze cut by a snakelike canal. By train the effect is muted. *Mestre*, the long bridgeway, the concrete and glass *Stazione Termine*. The best is by sea: a measured approach, *adagio*, the still lagoon, a wooden pile and a lone hut, *adagio*, the city a violet apparition hovering on the horizon, *adagio, adagietto*, a long curving line of *bricoli*. I am almost there. The spires are ever closer. I am almost inside.

Each time, at the moment of arrival, when the doors of the airplane are opened and I stand at the top of the stairs, when I drop my bags in the railway station and run to the glass doors for that first magic view, when the boat docks and I step off, I realize I have made a

mistake. I cannot enter the comfort of the laby-
rinth. I have taken a wrong turn. I am faced
with broad empty streets, windswept and
dusty: Lethbridge, Medicine Hat, Brooks. I
have never actually visited these towns, but in
my dreams I visit them endlessly.

Over the last few years the stretch of time
between these dreams grew longer and longer.
Until the day I received your mother's letter.
You were ill and in need. But you were locked
away from me, trapped in the centre of a
Venetian maze. The dreams filled my nights,
stacking up on top of each other, one over the
other, until I was so weighed down I could
barely lift my head from the pillow.

I do not own all the dreams and memories
I must carry. When I was a child, Papa would
deflect any of my questions about the war. He
would tell a humorous story — the night all
the officers got drunk, the day the company
geese went missing — but I sensed his holding
me off. Likewise Mamma, usually so free with
her stories, became hesitant. 'Best not to think
of it. If you knew. The misery.'

But when they were with friends, the other
few from the Veneto, I caught glimpses. Late
at night, after much homemade wine had been
drunk and all the younger children had fallen
asleep, they sang and they talked. One man in
particular, one I was rather afraid of, for he
was loud and sharp. *Sempre scattando* — his

nerves always shooting, as Mamma would say. He would start it. He'd been with the partisans.

> *O partigiano*
> *portami via*
> *O bella ciao, bella ciao*
> *Bella ciao, ciao, ciao*
> *O partigiano*
> *portami via*
> *che me sento di morir*

> (Oh partisans
> take me away with you
> goodbye, my pretty one
> goodbye
> oh partisans
> take me away
> for I feel I am to die)

To survive, he'd had to lie with the dead, lie between the bodies for twelve hours. Worse, in rage and terror, he had helped ambush and kill. 'I never touched a gun again after that. Never. And I never will. Even when they drafted me I refused. That's why I came here.'

Each one of them had his story: dangers escaped and atrocities witnessed. The innocent had been executed and the guilty had flourished. Even Mamma had been forced to watch an SS officer shoot ten young boys, chosen at random, watch ten young bodies drop into the canal.

From my position, on the periphery, I found the way the stories were told, the expression, as upsetting as the details. My mother, my father, my parents' friends, each of them became someone else, someone unknown, as he told his tale. Hands and voices shook, tears appeared suddenly, just as suddenly to be replaced by harsh laughter. Their distress, their impotent frustration, made them alien, connected to the violence they recalled. I was fascinated and afraid, wanting and not wanting to hear.

Sempre semplice, you said. But is this not why? No memories of war and slaughter have tattooed themselves on my brain. I have not been stained with spilt blood, and I harbour no hidden stories.

Simple?

I sit in my book-stuffed study and write. Struggling with words, facts, opinions, the fragments of events that come through the family letters, the phone calls, to find the significant order, the hidden truth. It is late spring. The sun is higher in the sky. The winter passed gently. There was little need this year for armouring oneself in preparation. Besides, I was like a hibernating animal, hiding out here in my little house, noticing now and then the depth of snow, the length of daylight, but turning back always to the words, to you.

I see clearly the yellowish white walls of your hospital room. A good hospital, an expensive hospital, I'm told. You are allowed books, a television, but they do not tempt you. You are too far away. You lie for hours, arms limply at your side, or you pace ritualistically wall to wall, back and forth. They say, the cold-eyed doctors, that you are improving, that the drugs are working, that soon you will be able to go home, that you have even gained weight. (The flesh hanging soft and alien on your bones.)

They needed no scalpel this time, no violence, only the gentleness of pills and injections. They took the anguish. They took the edge from your voice. So when Paola comes, as she eventually will, you'll be able to beg. Another chance. Francesco.

While, for me, the time has come to end this hiding away. The connections have been made and the context developed. Last week, the television, the late night national news, presented me with one of those rare moments of linkage, one of those moments when different truths intersect. Knowlton Nash, sincere and serious newsman, announced the opening in Rome of the trial of a group of terrorists. The short bit of film showed several of the accused entering the courthouse and then the whole group in a cage in the courtroom. They looked so Italian, all of them — cocky, handsome, and stylishly dressed. Several smiled intimately at the camera. They seemed on the verge of winking an eye, shrugging a shoulder, tossing off a 'what did you expect?' Instead, they clasped fists and chanted insults. And, in the centre of this well-featured, handsome group, in the centre of the cage, there was a silent, unmoving man. Piero. He was on the screen for just a few seconds, but I knew the face and the menace.

This week, Barbara arrived and I must play the wise aunt with a trunkful of distractions. Poor child — as I write she is standing in the living room, staring out the window at the still leafless trees and mud-filled garden, wondering what place this is. I see a part of both my and your childhood selves in her wondering, fearful eyes.

So I begin again my life in this city, this land. City: the place where the citizen is at home. I will, with the others, make this city, imagine it fully. The possibility exists. We are not yet confined by old fantasies and old blood, all the weight of what has already been done, good and bad. In our simplicity we are unhampered, untried. The energy can run free.

The possibility exists, in spite of the thoughtless vulgarity of public life and celebration, in spite of the tiresome boosterism, sign of how much Edmonton is at its insecure beginning. The possibility, I saw it, felt it one summer evening last year as I walked with a friend in the river valley. The tree-lined paths, the grassy knolls were crowded, overrun with gangs of youths and restless families. Seeing so many people out walking at night, that alone evoked Europe. But both my companion and I were cynical, irritated, as were those milling people. I heard their complaints as they pushed and passed in the dark, of the waste of money, the need for a multitude of practical services. We had all come to see the turning on of an artificial waterfall from a metal bridge spanning the valley to the river below. We had all come prepared, I suspect, to jeer a bit and, when the first few weak trickles of water were spotted, a groan did pass between us. But then the water began to fall in full force, then a splendid white veil spread from the black bridge. There was a long moment of silence before the cheers rang out — a moment when all of us in that valley were united in surprise and awe, a work of public art for us.

I thought of your watery city that evening, 'founded', Machiavelli said, by 'a people who left an agreeable and fertile country to occupy one sterile and unwholesome,' a people who, through their industriousness and will created joy from a barren marsh. And I began to believe that the people around me and, yes, I, could also shape these vast spaces, could also learn the habit of art. What we could make with our gain.

Why have I spent my winter telling your story? I needed to exorcise my dream of Venice. I needed to rid myself of the ache of longing that I have carried for so long. And you —

you are the grain of sand that began the pearl that is my dream.

Once during that special summer so many years ago, you kissed me. I heard that you had hurt yourself, slipped, fallen, and hit your head on some beach rocks. I arrived at your room looking, you told me, paler than you. I was shaking with concern. Smiling, you drew me to you. I felt your arms around me, your chest against mine. Then, then, your lips met mine. The spell of childhood was broken. I was awakened.

So many years ago. You are no longer my Prince Charming with your theatrical disillusion, your dated, alienated young man role. But you cut the pattern of my desire, so it is the skeptical, the ironical and, above all, the thin — the feel of bone just under the skin — that captures my interest.

I was never of any importance to you. If I could touch you as you did me. If I could help you now when you need help, when you need. But I am here and you there. You are a Venetian. How can you not feel the exhaustion, the decay of the world? My kiss — hopeful and Canadian — could never awaken you from your sleep of negativism.

Once I tried to lecture you through my usual medium. I retold a story. I used O'Connor's 'Good Country People' to warn you of the dangers of thinking you believed in nothing.

Printed by
Ateliers Graphiques Marc Veilleux Inc.
Cap-Saint-Ignace (Québec)
in September 1993

'Stories,' you said. 'With you it's always stories. I'm talking of my life.'

With me, it is always stories. And in the end it is all I can offer you — your story. I recreate your infancy, your childhood, trying to understand. I imagine the bombings, the operation. I look out through your eyes. I become you. I make the story, the book.

Still. Still I cannot write it in Italian, and you do not read English. I will never touch you at all.